FOREIGN POLICY
IN AMERICAN GOVERNMENT

INTRODUCTORY READERS IN AMERICAN POLITICS

FOREIGN POLICY
IN AMERICAN GOVERNMENT

Readings Selected and Edited

by BERNARD C. COHEN *The University of Wisconsin*

LITTLE, BROWN AND COMPANY
Boston • Toronto

FIRST PRINTING

*Published simultaneously in Canada
by Little, Brown & Company (Canada) Limited*

PRINTED IN THE UNITED STATES OF AMERICA

Contents

EDITOR'S INTRODUCTION vii

I. ISSUES AND PROBLEMS
     IN AMERICAN FOREIGN POLICY

1. New Dimensions in American Foreign Policy 3
   BERNARD C. COHEN

2. The Nuclear Test Ban Treaty: Two Views 19
   DEAN RUSK *The Secretary of State Defends
     the Test Ban Treaty* 20
   EDWARD TELLER *An Eminent Scientist Questions
     the Test Ban Treaty* 30

II. THE EXECUTIVE BRANCH

3. The Presidency 47
   RICHARD E. NEUSTADT *The Presidency, the Executive Branch,
     and National Security* 48

4. The Department of State 62
   CHARLTON OGBURN, JR. *The Flow of Policymaking
     in the Department of State* 63

5. Personnel for the New Diplomacy 74
   COMMITTEE ON FOREIGN AFFAIRS PERSONNEL *The Kinds
     and Attributes of Personnel* 75

6. The National Security Council 88
   BURTON M. SAPIN *The Organization and Procedures
     of the National Security Council Mechanism* 89

III. SPECIALIZED FUNCTIONS

7. Intelligence 111
   ROBERTA WOHLSTETTER *Surprise* 111

8. Planning in Foreign Policy 126
   FRANKLIN A. LINDSAY *Program Planning:
   The Missing Element* 127

9. Expert Advice: The Scientist as Policy Adviser 139
   ALBERT WOHLSTETTER *Scientists, Seers and Strategy* . . . 140

IV. CONTEXTS AND CONSTITUENTS

10. Congress 157
    COMMITTEE ON FOREIGN RELATIONS, UNITED STATES SENATE
    The Foreign Assistance Act of 1961 158
    RAYMOND A. BAUER, ITHIEL DE SOLA POOL, AND
    LEWIS ANTHONY DEXTER *The Job of the Congressman* . 170

11. Interest Groups 182
    RAYMOND A. BAUER, ITHIEL DE SOLA POOL, AND
    LEWIS ANTHONY DEXTER *Communications — Pressure,
    Influence, or Education?* 182

12. The Press 194
    BERNARD C. COHEN *The Press and Foreign Policy
    in the United States* 194

Editor's Introduction

The institutions of American government and politics take on life and texture as they come to grips with current questions of public policy. Whether these are matters having to do with education or labor, agriculture or foreign trade, military security or civil rights, foreign policy or public welfare, the processes of hammering out an acceptable piece of national legislation or a statement of governmental intentions reveal our political institutions — not in some ideal textbook condition, but rather in their workaday configuration. Different areas of policy serve to illuminate different aspects of different institutions, and thus a full understanding of American government requires exploration of a wide range of public policy questions.

There is a disposition among students of American government to look a little more closely at foreign policy than at other policy areas, not because it affords special insight into the American political system, but because foreign policy questions, having "life or death" qualities, are judged to be more important, more fundamental, than other questions of public policy. Because foreign policy is accorded priority in this normative sense, it is given priority in the political system itself and also in the study of that system. What the latter gives us is not special insight so much as different insight, in the sense that the things it tells us about the political system are not always the same things we learn from a comparable study of the more numerous areas of "domestic" public policy.

In the articles that follow, we want to look both at the characteristics of foreign policy as a kind of public policy, and at the particular bearing foreign policy has on American political institutions. In a collection of this kind, there is always a question concerning the appropriate balance between material on substantive foreign policy matters and material on the way those matters are handled in our political institutions. I have "gone light," so to speak, on the former for two reasons: First, substantive discussions of foreign policy do not speak for themselves insofar as their implications for American government and politics are concerned — a large number of such articles would still require that their implications be drawn out and made explicit; and in the second place — as I argue in the introduction to the readings on the nuclear test ban treaty — it is hard to preserve the timeliness and relevance of foreign policy discussions. Therefore, I have limited the consideration of the substantive aspects of American foreign policy to a general essay on the characteristics and implications of contemporary foreign policy problems, and to a pro-and-con discussion of the merits of the nuclear test ban treaty. The readings then explore in some detail the way in which foreign policy questions are handled in the American political system.

I am grateful to the authors and publishers of these articles for their permission to reprint; specific acknowledgments are made at appropriate places in the text. I also want to thank Donald R. Hammonds of Little, Brown and Company for his help and encouragement; this volume is testimony to his winning ways.

I

ISSUES AND PROBLEMS
IN AMERICAN FOREIGN POLICY

1   *New Dimensions in American Foreign Policy*

BERNARD C. COHEN

In the years since the Second World War, foreign policy has emerged as the chief concern of the United States government. While we are now coming to recognize that circumstance as normal, it was not always so; in fact, the famed "return to normalcy" after the First World War was an explicit rejection of foreign policy in favor of the parochial domestic preoccupations that had characterized American politics for much of the nineteenth century. The new normalcy of international involvement is having important effects on many aspects of American political life, and thus it compels our attention as a major energizer and shaper of our political institutions and our political behavior.

The priority given to foreign policy by present-day Administrations is evident in such obvious indicators as the daily preoccupations of officials and the patterns of expenditure at the national level; and it is increasingly reflected in the behavior of candidates for highest office. Although the newspaper filters reality in ways that are not always obvious, even a casual reader of the daily press gains a sense of how heavily the external world weighs on the shoulders of the American President and his chief advisers, and how much of their time they allocate to foreign affairs. Yet the press perhaps underplays the preoccupation with foreign affairs, since many of its manifestations, the regular intelligence briefings on international developments, for example, are both secret and not "news" in the prevailing judgment of reporters. At times the White House becomes so absorbed in its international problems that it lets slide the many issues of domestic policy and politics that are also pressing for settlement. In one such period early in the Kennedy Administration a

3

major columnist, having in mind the "equal-time" provisions of the
Federal Communications Act regarding free political broadcasts,
suggested that the President ought to give equal time to domestic
policy matters.

In budgetary terms, the claims of foreign policy and of our international obligations are equally as great, and perhaps more readily
visible. Fully half of the budget of the Federal government goes for
national defense expenditures, which support the military posture
that sustains American political and security interests in the world.
Additional billions of dollars are spent on the Atomic Energy Commission's program, on the foreign aid program, on the work of the
Department of State, the United States Information Agency, and
aspects of the work of other departments and agencies like Commerce and Labor that have international interests and maintain
representatives abroad. Additional billions are spent in payment of
the costs of international involvements in the past, such as veterans'
benefits and the interest payments on national indebtedness stemming from the financing of past wars. These costs are easy to pull
together and to measure; more difficult is estimating the cost of our
international commitments and policies in terms of the alternative
domestic policies — in education, for example, or health and welfare,
or highways and transportation — that we might have afforded had
we not been so deeply committed elsewhere.

The claims of foreign policy and of national security on the time
and attention of our national leaders are so great and so compelling
that they influence the selection and behavior of Presidential candidates and, beyond that, the outcome of these elections. Many factors
actually impinge on the voting decisions of individual citizens, and
specific judgments concerning the policy positions of individual
candidates are only a minor aspect of these factors; yet in combination with more generalized impressions of the over-all competence
of candidates to handle "the problems of the world," so to speak, they
are significant enough to be regarded as contributing elements in
the outcome of elections.[1] In the belief that this is the case, political
parties and individual candidates plan their strategies and make
their decisions; and in the process they help to confirm the expectation. Since the Second World War every major contender for the
Presidency has consciously tried to present himself as a statesman, a

[1] Cf. A. Campbell, P. Converse, W. Miller, and D. Stokes, *The American
Voter* (New York: John Wiley & Sons, Inc., 1960).

man who can deal effectively with the leaders of other nations and solve the pressing foreign policy problems of the day. Some candidates have had what others thought were strange views on *how* the problems might be solved, but nonetheless they did have views which were a prominent part of their image. On the other hand, no man has gotten the nomination of a major political party in this period who has dismissed foreign policy, or deprecated his own abilities to handle it — as did a Presidential hopeful in 1960 who stemmed (forever!) a tide of reporters' questions on foreign affairs with the remark, "Why do you ask me these things? All I know about foreign affairs is what I read in *The New York Times*."

I

Why has this happened? How has it come about that the United States has acquired worldwide obligations and interests having such pervasive consequences for everyday life, private as well as political? Through most of the nineteenth century and for a part of the twentieth the United States was effectively insulated against most of the political–military pressures originating in Europe, by virtue of its geographical location, the prevailing state of military technology, and a favorable balance, or distribution, of power among the major nations. As a consequence of these three interrelated factors, little power could be mobilized for effective employment in transoceanic adventures, and the United States was free to concentrate on internal problems.

By the time the Second World War had ended, however, the complex factors that contribute to national power had been subjected, in almost every country, to radical change. Most of the victors as well as the vanquished in that war — the most powerful nations of the nineteenth-century world — were exhausted, their resources and their capabilities scarcely adequate to cope with the challenge of reconstruction. Two countries emerged with impressive power and political will intact: The United States, no longer so well protected by geography or technology, found itself face to face with a new threat posed by the political ambitions of the Soviet Union, while it was the only one of the Western powers able to stand up to this threat and contain it.

At that moment a scientific and technological revolution overtook the industrial revolution in warfare; from that point on, the scientists and engineers rather than the assembly lines held the key to large-scale military power. The consequences of this transformation have kept the United States in the exposed position of leadership and responsibility in which she found herself at the end of the Second World War. For one thing, the great cost of nuclear military capabilities has severely limited the number of nations that could effectively compete in this realm, at least at the level set by the United States.[2] A single statistic may give some idea of what it means to run an atomic weapons program of the size of our own: Over extended periods of time the U.S. Atomic Energy Commission has consumed as much as 10 per cent of the total production of electricity in the United States. In a competition of this order, the United States and the Soviet Union have set the pace for each other; the gap between these two and other existing or would-be nuclear powers is so great that it is not likely to be closed for a long time to come, and certainly not without great effort and possibly great innovations.

The United States has remained at a high level of involvement for yet another reason inherent in the new military technology: For the first time in the history of this nation, we have become directly vulnerable to large-scale, potentially decisive, military attack. Science and technology, applied to military strategy, have obliterated the protective effects of distance, time, and localized balances of power, on which our security depended for so long. Intercontinental missiles carrying nuclear warheads have put us on the firing line, so to speak, and have involved us deeply in the effort to construct a stable order of world power — just as the great powers of the nineteenth century were so involved during the years of America's internal preoccupations.[3]

In this new international setting, then, the United States accepted a twofold role: It was simultaneously the chief deterrer of military and political expansion by the Soviet Union and its Communist allies, and the creator and leader of a new Western coalition designed to restore military and political strength and some unity of

[2] But it should be noted that what countries can "afford" depends on what they think it worthwhile to allocate their resources to; the strain has been great on the Soviets, too, no doubt, but their international ambitions were large enough to justify the cost. It should also be pointed out that one of the rationales behind the French nuclear weapons program is the belief that a nation can compete "effectively" with a much smaller nuclear establishment than the Russians possess — a complex and controversial argument.

[3] Cf. Bernard Brodie, *Strategy in the Missile Age* (Princeton: Princeton University Press, 1959).

action to the countries of Western Europe. As Chief Deterrer, the United States has felt it necessary to stand in the way of Communist expansion around the world, from Iran in 1946 to South Vietnam in 1965, by means as diverse as United Nations political action, limited warfare, economic aid, strategic deterrence involving the threat of nuclear retaliation, and tactical airlifts. And as Coalition Leader, the United States led in the development of NATO, the first peacetime military alliance this country has ever joined, and has encouraged other forms of European economic, political, and military integration.[4]

In the first decade after the Second World War, these two roles were unambiguous; the contrast between Communist aggressiveness and general Western weakness was so obviously striking that American policies were not seriously challenged either at home or throughout the Western world. Since the mid-1950's, however, changes in world power and policy have been so great as to evoke widespread questioning of these basic policies and approaches, and to stimulate a search for new political arrangements for a less obviously "bipolar" world. Five of these changes in the alignment of forces in the world deserve special attention.

First, there has been a fundamental change in the basic strategic situation between East and West. In the first postwar decade the United States had either a monopoly of nuclear weapons or an overwhelming superiority. Its arrangements with its NATO allies and its military posture vis-à-vis the Soviet Union were both designed in the knowledge that this country, and this country alone, possessed this unquestioned and untouchable power. The second postwar decade has brought this unique superiority to an end; the Soviet Union has now achieved an approximate parity with the United States in strategic nuclear power.

The new vulnerability of the United States to nuclear attack from the Soviet Union has been the occasion, though not the sole cause, for a *second* change: Doubts among some Europeans about the willingness of the United States to rush to the defense of European countries now that the United States might itself suffer retaliation, together with the renewed economic vitality of Europe, have led to a challenge to the American monopoly of leadership and especially of nuclear control within the Alliance. France under President de

---

[4] Cf. John W. Spanier, *American Foreign Policy Since World War II,* Revised edn. (New York: Frederick A. Praeger, Inc., 1962).

Gaulle has been particularly eager to minimize American influence on European policy, and is engaged in building its own nuclear deterrent force (*force de frappe*) as a substitute for reliance on the American, and hopefully as the nucleus of a European deterrent that will be wholly separate from that of the United States. Germany, which does not possess a nuclear force, and Great Britain, which does have one but which under the Labour Government would like to relinquish it to some wider Atlantic control, have interests of their own that are not the same as the French, making the search for a common ground even more difficult.

Third, the hostility and aggressiveness of the Soviet Union have abated somewhat, raising additional questions in the West about the appropriateness of international political and military arrangements that were constructed in the face of an implacable Soviet menace. This new moderation in Soviet behavior and policies, which bore early fruit in the nuclear test ban treaty in 1963, has several apparent causes. The Soviet bloc, like the Western, has felt the divisive effects of growing nationalism. Communist China has challenged the authority of the erstwhile undisputed leader of the bloc, and has won the support of a number of other Communist nations. Underlying this division is an apparent conflict of national interests: The Soviet Union has become more sensitive to the risks of continuing a policy of unrelieved hostility toward the United States as her political system has become more stable and her economy more fully developed. Having much to lose in any nuclear conflict, she now favors more restrained political and economic forms of competition with the capitalist world, while the Chinese see few unacceptable losses and the possibility of tremendous gains by pressing forward with undiminished militant revolutionary ardor. As a result, it is now less clear in the Western nations who the "real" enemy is, if indeed there is one any more, and what the meaning of these developments is for individual or for concerted Western policies.

Fourth, the search for a stable world order is additionally complicated by the emergence to independent status of many economically undeveloped and politically weak and unstable ex-colonies. The opening of the nineteenth United Nations General Assembly in November, 1964, saw three new nations admitted, for a total of 115, more than twice the original membership of 51. The large number of these new nations in the United Nations makes it increasingly less reliable as a forum for the handling of problems of central concern to the large powers. Furthermore, the conflicts within and among these new states offer enticing opportunities for an extension of great-power competitions, and they contain the ever-present possibility of disorder and disaster on a scale that could hardly help but engulf the great powers. Political stability on a world scale involves shared norms and predictable responses; and these attributes, hard to find or develop anywhere, are even less likely to appear in new countries whose political leadership is weak, inexperienced, and distrustful of most of the former colonial powers.[5]

Fifth, the impending spread of nuclear weapons among increasing numbers of nations is threatening to dissolve whatever elements of stability and security have been won at such great expense in the past 20 years. Five countries now have nuclear weapons stockpiles and/or programs: the United States, the Soviet Union, Britain, France, and Communist China. Officials in other countries who have close and competitive contacts with some of these nuclear powers — India, for example — are beginning to wonder out loud whether the time has come for them to develop nuclear weapons also. "Nuclear proliferation" has now become a matter of grave concern to the United States and, in the light of Chinese developments, possibly to the Soviet Union as well. Partly this is the nervousness of those who are reluctant to part with the political advantages of a well-established oligopoly; but the nervousness is due also to the knowledge of how difficult and costly it is to ensure positive control over nuclear weapons and delivery systems, and to the associated fear that the use of nuclear weapons anywhere in the world might spread very quickly to all the nuclear powers.

All the circumstances, thus, of the 20 years since the end of the Second World War have worked to keep the United States in the forefront of world politics, and to put on her shoulders an extraordinary responsibility for the development and the maintenance of what we now have in the way of a free and stable world order. If the problems of the late 1940's and the 1950's were of great historic import, those of the 1960's are more subtle and complex — and no less dangerous. With a multiplicity of conflicting goals, with political alignments criss-crossing on a number of issues, and with accustomed political means seemingly having reached the point of diminishing

[5] Cf. Peter Calvocoressi, *World Order and New States* (London: Chatto & Windus for The Institute for Strategic Studies, 1962).

returns, foreign policy decision-making is an increasingly difficult political endeavor.

II

We have been considering, in the preceding section, the modern setting for American foreign policy. Now we have to ask, what is the significance of this foreign policy position for American government and politics? We shall try to answer this question by looking first at some characteristics of contemporary foreign policy questions, and then in the final section at some characteristics of the political processes that have evolved to cope with these problems. After that, the selected readings will further explore some aspects of the foreign policy-making process in detail.

One of the more obvious of the substantive characteristics of contemporary foreign policy is the tremendous *complexity* of the questions themselves. We are confronted today not only with the familiar complexity of large numbers of competing interests, where the processes of accommodation require substantial skill and adroitness — if indeed an acceptable reconciliation of divergent interests is even possible. We are also dealing with questions involving new techniques or institutions or technologies, where the ramifications or consequences are unfamiliar or even impossible to foresee or disentangle. The extensive literature on nuclear deterrence suggests the complexities involved in a highly technical subject matter where the relevant assumptions about behavior in critical situations must remain untested, and the major conclusions can be at best only very disciplined speculations.[6]

A second characteristic of the issues is the *darkness,* so to speak, that surrounds them. The ordinary difficulties of mobilizing energies and organizing support for the attainment of goals are compounded when central elements of information are lacking or even unobtainable. This missing information may concern the behavior of the people we are dealing with — their intentions, their expectations, their beliefs and aspirations, their modes of responding to the moves of others. It may concern the capabilities of other countries or their statesmen — their political or technical capacities to sustain a given action. Or it may involve actual events, as in a number of instances

[6] Cf. Herman Kahn, *On Thermonuclear War* (Princeton: Princeton University Press, 1960); Glenn H. Snyder, *Deterrence and Defense* (Princeton: Princeton University Press, 1961).

involving alleged Communist Pathet Lao movements in Laos or North Vietnamese raids in and around South Vietnam where the American government has been uninformed or misinformed about happenings.

A third characteristic, equally obvious, relates to the *high stakes* of foreign policy today: the high cost of many modern policies, and the possibly even higher risks that surround them. The impact of foreign policy upon the federal budget, which was mentioned at the start of this essay, is testimony to the high dollar cost as well as the opportunity costs of — i.e., alternative opportunities foregone as a result of — the choices we make. But dollar costs are not likely to be unsupportable for a rich country like the United States, whereas the risks can be overwhelming in their magnitude. The Cuban episode of 1962, for example, was not a very costly enterprise, but the risk of nuclear war hung on every step that was taken and every word that was said. Similar risks lurk in the shadows of every sharp confrontation between the United States and the Soviet Union and even indirect or muted conflicts contain the seeds of a possible escalation to a point where the risks of open war become relevant. Long-range risks are disturbing also, such as those associated with a world of 15 or 20 nuclear powers, wherein weapons could be bought and sold as well as made. A portion of this risk attaches to all policies, even scientific and commercial policies on reactors, that contribute to such a situation, as well as to failures to take actions that might defer it.

These characteristics can be better illustrated by a closer look at a few contemporary issues. Let us consider, first of all, the matter of foreign aid, which has been a fixed part of United States foreign policy in one format or another and for one purpose or another for 20 years.

The chief purpose of American economic assistance abroad at the present time and for some years back has been to facilitate the economic development of underdeveloped areas. Behind this economic objective has been a political one: Economic development is viewed as the necessary foundation for "political development" — that is, political stability and the nurturance of democratic political institutions. Stable democracies, it is reasoned, cannot develop in traditionally oriented, poverty-ridden societies, where aspirations are limited, education is scarce, and little energy is left over from the search for subsistence to devote to the tasks of self-government.

Foreign aid is thus regarded as an investment in future world order; but the need for such assistance is felt in the present, and the reluctant competition between the Communist nations and the Western nations to gain short-run political advantage by being the benefactor who responds to these needs is also part of the current international political scene.[7]

The long-term advantages of foreign aid have long been an article of faith for those people who have been trying to construct a stable, free international political system. Yet a decade of experience is now throwing into question the axioms on which this faith has rested. Both sides in the world conflict have spent billions of dollars for economic aid, with no appreciable gains in many instances in terms of economic growth or political stability or even political friendship or orientation. Thus the very sequence of causal relationships is cast in doubt: (1) Economic aid does not necessarily lead to appreciable economic growth or development; much hinges on social and cultural attitudes, on the nature of the investment, on related economic activities, on the growth of the population, and so forth. (2) Economic development does not necessarily lead to political stability; the mechanisms involved here are not well understood, but it seems clear that where growth does take place, there may be an associated rise in the level and intensity of political activity which may be destabilizing rather than stabilizing. (3) Political stability is not the same thing as political democracy, nor does it necessarily lead to political democracy. In fact, there has been a pronounced tendency in the underdeveloped countries for stability to be achieved at the expense of democratic institutions and practices. (4) Democracy, where it does exist, does not necessarily conduce to international peace and stability. The Wilsonian belief that democratic nations are peaceful nations has long since been proved false.[8]

In these circumstances, policy problems that involve questions of economic aid can be seen to display most of the characteristics discussed above. The dollar costs are of course high; so are the political costs for administration leaders and congressmen as they perceive an apparent unpopularity for foreign aid in certain constituencies.

[7] Cf. Max F. Millikan and Donald L. M. Blackmer, eds., *The Emerging Nations* (Boston: Little, Brown, 1961).

[8] Cf. Edward C. Banfield, "American Foreign Aid Doctrines," in Robert A. Goldwin, ed., *Why Foreign Aid?* (Chicago: Rand McNally & Co., 1963).

The risks of conflict are of course very low, which is one of the attractive features of this form of international competition; but the risks of failure — which is to say, the risks of both economic loss and the more important political loss if foreign aid has been the chief reliance of our diplomacy — are high. The issues involved are, furthermore, of extreme complexity, in the sense that countless cultural, social, economic, and political variables must be taken into consideration, while causal connections are obscure and political consequences are especially difficult to predict or control. Lastly, while available information on the economy and society may be easy to obtain, much of the information that would be relevant to any decision (e.g., information on future behavior, or on actions in the present in other political, social, or economic spheres) is often simply not available.

The "control" of nuclear weapons, a problem that manifests itself in several foreign policy issues, also serves to illustrate these substantive characteristics of policy in the 1960's. Efforts to contain the spread of nuclear weapons and to limit their possible use now involve us in separate questions of policy with the Soviet Union and also with our NATO allies.

With respect to the Soviets the problem has long been conceived of as finding ways to slow down or de-fuse the nuclear competition between the two great nuclear powers, and simultaneously getting these two powers to cooperate to discourage the development of nuclear weapons by other countries. This task was a fruitless one for many years, for the basic reason that nuclear weapons were too important to the central strategies of both sides for them to halt the processes of development and acquisition before "adequate" numbers and varieties of such weapons had been stockpiled. Arguments that the United States and the Soviet Union had a "common interest" in self-denying measures that would also block the spread of nuclear weapons to additional countries always broke down before the patent demonstration that each of the two major nations had a prior national interest in insuring the adequacy of its own weapons. In a situation of nuclear plenty, however, both sides began to see more advantage in general policies of nuclear restriction and restraint than in unlimited development programs. From 1958 to 1961 an informal, tacit ban on tests of nuclear weapons was in effect for the United States, Great Britain, and the Soviet Union, with much uneasiness and suspicion on both sides. After the French government began to test its newly developed weapons in the Sahara, the Soviets used the French action as a justification for their sudden resumption of tests, and the United States government followed suit some months later. After the Cuban crisis in the fall of 1962, however, both the United States and the Soviet Union made a major effort to "step back from the brink." The first result of this new turn was the so-called "hot line," a direct communications link between the White House and the Kremlin. The second product was the nuclear test ban treaty of 1963 (now signed by over a hundred nations, excluding France and Communist China), which codified the maximum amount of agreement thus far achieved by the two nations: an officially uninspected ban on nuclear tests in the three environments (atmosphere, underwater, and outer space) where *unilateral* inspection is adequate to detect violations. Testing still goes on in underground sites, as does the search for reliable and acceptable means of detection and inspection of underground tests.

The measures so far taken and proposals for additional measures that would ban tests, or cut back production of nuclear materials, or monitor the peaceful uses of outer space, all raise an acute dilemma. On one horn of this dilemma sit the risks of unrestrained nuclear development, including a sharpening of the nuclear rivalry between the United States and the Soviet Union (carrying with it the increased possibility of accidental, unauthorized, or unintended use of nuclear weapons), and an increase in the number of nuclear powers (for whom testing is an indispensable forerunner of nuclear weapons production). On the other horn perches the risk that the kind of agreements that are currently obtainable with the Soviet Union jeopardize the security position of the United States by interfering with the development of our still-imperfect offensive and defensive capabilities, and by allowing the Soviet Union to escape the obligations of a formal inspection system. Each of these risks arises out of problems of unimagined complexity — the problem of strategic deterrence, and all the related questions of reasonable or probable (as well as unforeseeable) behavior on the part of nations that respond simultaneously to pressures both to cooperate and to oppose. And in the background is the question of France and Communist China, whose unwillingness to cooperate in measures of nuclear control may eventually raise the risks of restraint for both the United States and the Soviet Union to a point where they are greater than the risks of renewed nuclear competition.[9]

With respect to our NATO allies, the "control" problem may be defined as one of finding mutually satisfactory ways to give the Europeans a greater share in decisions involving nuclear weapons while retaining for ourselves the centralized and final authority. Many Europeans, as we noted earlier, have come to disbelieve our recurrent promises that we will use our nuclear force against the Russians if they should launch an attack on Europe. The doubters reason that our resolve to strike the Russians, no matter how firm it may be at the present time, will crumble at the moment of decision when we confront the imminent prospect of a Soviet nuclear counter-blow against our own cities. Some Europeans want to remove the element of doubt by institutional devices that would allow them to participate in decisions concerning the use or the non-use of nuclear weapons in the interests of the whole alliance. Others, notably the French, regard such institutional mechanisms as rationalizations for continued United States control over nuclear decision-making, and argue that the only truly reliable way of guaranteeing that they can dispose of nuclear weapons in their own defense is to have their own nuclear weapons.[10]

The United States in this situation is extremely reluctant to give away the ultimate control it has maintained over the use of nuclear weapons in NATO strategy. But it is equally reluctant to see any European nations develop their own strategic nuclear forces. It means too many independent triggers to nuclear war, too many resources diverted away from what it believes to be the more pressing task of providing for the non-nuclear defense of Europe, too great an incentive ultimately for the Germans to acquire a nuclear force of their own, with all the adverse effects that would have on Soviet policy and on the other NATO nations too. The United States "solution" to this problem has been the proposed multilateral force (MLF), a surface fleet armed with Polaris missiles, manned by

[9] Cf. Hedley Bull, *The Control of the Arms Race* (London: Weidenfeld and Nicolson for The Institute for Strategic Studies, 1961); Thomas C. Schelling and Morton H. Halperin, *Strategy and Arms Control* (New York: The Twentieth Century Fund, 1961).

[10] Cf. Alastair Buchan, *NATO in the 1960's*, Revised edn. (New York: Frederick A. Praeger, 1963); Alastair Buchan and Philip Windsor, *Arms and Stability in Europe* (London: Chatto & Windus for The Institute for Strategic Studies, 1963).

mixed crews drawn from the naval forces of the member countries in the Alliance. The MLF would give Europeans a larger voice in the nuclear protection of Europe, but still not a controlling voice.

The American advocacy of the mixed-manned principle has perhaps compounded the problems of the NATO alliance rather than resolved them. Strong French opposition to the proposal, and the lack of enthusiasm in Great Britain and other countries have left the United States and Germany exposed in their commitment to it and to each other. The Soviets are arguing that the MLF will give Germany access to nuclear weapons, and thus encourage rather than discourage nuclear proliferation. A proposal which was meant to solve a political rather than a strategic problem has widened the political fissures in the Alliance. To the issues of nuclear reliability and control, then, have been added a host of questions involving United States relations with its European allies, intra-European (most notably Franco-German) relations, and the future of NATO itself. The complexities here are enormous, and the competing interests run so deep that the costs and risks of *any* settlement seem likely to be uncomfortably high.

III

Finally, what can we say about the impact of these kinds of foreign policy questions on the processes of policy-making? What are some of the characteristics of the political processes that take shape around foreign policy issues? We shall take note of three important and far-reaching characteristics, each of which differs in greater or less degree from the processes that are apparent in questions of "domestic" politics and policies.

In the first place, there is a strong and visible reluctance on the part of foreign policy officials to rush into decisions or commitments. Where domestic politics occasionally involve — and even encourage — the formulation of bold new programs, the excessive dangers of the foreign policy arena develop a caution and conservatism on the part of those who are responsible for decisions. Policy officials will generally prefer the known and familiar to the unknown, even when the former is distasteful for one reason or another. Changes in content and/or direction of foreign policy are generally forced by events or demands originating in the outside world rather than in new preferences of American policy-makers. (The foreign policy innovations in the 1945–1950 period were fundamentally revolutionary in nature, taking cognizance of America's new position of world leadership, and were thus exceptional. Yet even these changes were collectively triggered by an external event — the Soviet threat.) The frequent criticisms of United States foreign policy that it is reactive and perhaps also reactionary draw much of their fuel from these cautionary tendencies. Where the peace of the world is thought to be involved, the pressure not to "rock the boat" is keenly felt.[11]

Secondly, the substantive characteristics of these policy questions have combined to endow the Executive branch of the government with great freedom of action vis-à-vis the Congress. Congressmen are political specialists, in the first instance, rather than subject-matter specialists; members and staffs of particular committees do develop considerable competence in foreign affairs and national security issues as compared with the average congressman, but this is on a small scale compared to the specialized abilities found among personnel in the Executive branch. The intricacies of the problems, the requirements for special kinds of information, and the concern for both external and internal security, all give the Executive a great and acknowledged advantage over the Legislature in the handling of foreign policy. And the congressman, too, does not want to go out of his way to accept responsibility for high-risk decisions, especially when he lacks the special knowledge and competence to do an adequate job on them. The more crucial the foreign policy issue, consequently, and the greater the likelihood of war risks, the more likely is the Congress to lapse into silence in the name of national unity, yielding all initiative to the Executive branch and disavowing for the moment even the role of critic.[12]

Thirdly, the factors and characteristics that constrain the effective powers of Congress vis-à-vis the Executive also work to modify the role of public opinion in the foreign policy field. Complexity, detail,

[11] And a slight rocking motion is widely noticed: cf. the attention given to Senator J. W. Fulbright's foreign policy critique of March 25, 1964, published in revised form as Chapter 1 in Senator J. W. Fulbright, *Old Myths and New Realities* (New York: Random House, 1964).

[12] Cf. Samuel P. Huntington, *The Common Defense* (New York: Columbia University Press, 1961); James A. Robinson, *Congress and Foreign Policy-Making* (Homewood, Ill.: The Dorsey Press, Inc., 1962); Robert A. Dahl, *Congress and Foreign Policy* (New York: Harcourt, Brace & Co., 1950) (Paperback edition: New York: W. W. Norton & Co., 1964); Lewis Anthony Dexter, "Congressmen and the Making of Military Policy," in Robert L. Peabody and Nelson W. Polsby, eds., *New Perspectives on the House of Representatives* (Chicago: Rand McNally & Co., 1963).

and secrecy serve to discourage the average man from making a heavy personal investment of time and energy in foreign policy matters; and the high risks that are associated with these policies seem also to generate additional pressures to escape involvement. Thus, while many areas of domestic policy call forth an interested, active, and reasonably broadly based public, most foreign policy areas or issues activate only a small and narrowly based public. These differential involvements are manifest in data from public opinion polls, and in the activities of interest groups over a range of policy questions.[13] A corollary of widespread public disinterest in foreign policy is an increase in "specialist" activity. This is particularly the case in those foreign policy matters that have a large national-security component; "public opinion" is generally led in such matters by a small number of people who have the professional competence to engage in debate on highly technical subjects. Thus the scientist, for example, has come to have a larger voice in the shaping not only of weapons-development policies, but also of policies bearing on their deployment and use. And because strategy has an important bearing on our political relations with other countries, scientists and professional strategists both occupy positions of influence in the determination of foreign policy.[14]

Insofar as these characteristics thrust more power into fewer hands, they run contrary to the tendency for broader political participation and control that has been one of the themes of twentieth-century American democracy. Like a pair of horses trying to pull in different directions, issues of foreign and domestic policy exert contradictory pressures on the American political system. In these circumstances it is important to understand the nature of foreign policy formulation, the special demands it makes on the political environment here at home, and the kinds of skills and performances that might satisfy these demands without putting intolerable strain or tension on our political system.

[13] Cf. Gabriel A. Almond, *The American People and Foreign Policy*, 2nd edn. (New York: Frederick A. Praeger, 1961); James N. Rosenau, *Public Opinion and Foreign Policy* (New York: Random House, 1961).

[14] Cf. Robert Gilpin and Christopher Wright, eds., *Scientists and National Policy-Making* (New York: Columbia University Press, 1964).

2   *The Nuclear Test Ban Treaty: Two Views*

Foreign policy problems are subject to almost constant change; and the formulations and concerns of last month or last year, unless they were of historic import, are likely to seem out-of-date, mildly irrelevant to the issues and choices of today and tomorrow. For this reason it is difficult to select brief readings dealing with substantive questions of foreign policy; most selections will seem to illustrate the issues of a prior generation.

To resolve this difficulty, I have included only one such issue in these readings, and have included two points of view on it. The policy question is the consent of the Senate to the ratification of the nuclear test ban treaty of 1963, and I have chosen it for three reasons. In the first place, it is of historic import; and since its provisions have a bearing on our daily lives, it is of present and future import too. Second, many of the specific questions that were involved in the larger issue of a nuclear arms control agreement with the Soviet Union will be with us for many years, and quite possibly even in this same form. Third, these questions and this issue display a great many of the characteristics and raise a great many of the problems that were outlined in the introductory essay, some of which will come up again in more detail in the subsequent readings.

The two points of view on the treaty are those of Secretary of State Dean Rusk and Dr. Edward Teller of the University of California. The Secretary of State was the first witness to appear before the Senate Foreign Relations Committee when it opened its hearings on the treaty on August 12, 1963, and he outlined the provisions of the treaty and the political arguments of the Administration in concluding it. The following day Secretary of Defense Robert Mc-Namara put the treaty "in the context of our present military position," in a concise military analysis that, while not appropriate for inclusion in this volume, merits the attention of interested stu-

dents.[1] *On August 20, 1963, after all the official witnesses had appeared, Dr. Teller testified to his grave disquiet over the treaty, taking issue with both Secretary Rusk and Secretary McNamara. The arguments reprinted here bring to the forefront (1) the great complexity of the test ban question; (2) the urgency both of "nuclear proliferation" and of national defense; (3) the importance, as well as the difficulties, of acquiring correct intelligence and using it effectively; (4) the intimate involvement of military considerations in American foreign policy; (5) the role and character of scientific advice in both military and foreign policy matters; and (6) the problems of the congressman when he is confronted with conflicting advice from experts.*

[1] See Testimony of Hon. Robert S. McNamara, Secretary of Defense, *Nuclear Test Ban Treaty,* Hearings before the Committee on Foreign Relations, United States Senate, 88th Congress, 1st Session, U.S. Government Printing Office, Washington, D.C., 1963, pp. 97–203.

The Secretary of State Defends the Test Ban Treaty

DEAN RUSK

Secretary Rusk: Mr. Chairman and Senators, I very much appreciate the promptness with which the Senate is turning its attention to the matter before us. I do want to thank you, Mr. Chairman, for the remarks which you kindly addressed to me and should like to say it was a most invaluable thing for me and I think the Government of the United States to have you and other Members of the Senate with us on this trip. We appreciate that very much.

I appear here this morning to support the treaty banning nuclear weapon tests in the atmosphere, in outer space, and underwater.

Last week in Moscow the treaty was signed on behalf of the United States and the other original parties — the United Kingdom and the U.S.S.R. The Senate of the United States now has the con-

Statement of Hon. Dean Rusk, Secretary of State, *Nuclear Test Ban Treaty,* Hearings before the Committee on Foreign Relations, United States Senate, 88th Congress, 1st Session, U.S. Government Printing Office, Washington, D.C., 1963, pp. 10–20.

stitutional responsibility to examine this treaty with care so that it may give the President its advice and, I earnestly hope, its consent to a prompt ratification.

The President has given the treaty before you this morning an apt characterization. It is, he has said, "not the millenium . . . but it is an important first step . . . a step toward peace — a step toward reason — a step away from war."

Since 1789 the Senate has given its consent without reservation to the ratification of 943 treaties. I believe this may well prove, I say, it may well prove one of the most significant occasions for the exercise of that constitutional prerogative. I say "may" because it depends somewhat on how the future develops in regard to the possibilities of peace.

HISTORY OF U.S. EFFORT AT NUCLEAR CONTROLS

The United States, as the first nation to unleash the power of the atom, recognized from the beginning its awesome potentialities for good and evil. In the less than two decades since the first use of a nuclear weapon, the United States has worked continuously to achieve effective international controls so that the power of the atom might be committed to the improvement, rather than the destruction, of mankind. Disarmament, and the control of weapons, both nuclear and conventional, have been concerns of the highest priority for the three administrations that have borne responsibility for the great issues of peace and war during the atomic era.

Less than a year after the explosions at Hiroshima and Nagasaki, the United States presented its first comprehensive proposal for international control of the atom. As offered by Bernard Baruch at the first meeting of the United Nations Atomic Energy Commission on June 14, 1946, the plan called for the creation of an International Atomic Development Authority with responsibility for control of all atomic energy activities potentially dangerous to our security, with the power to control, inspect, and license all other atomic activities, and with the duty of fostering the beneficial uses of atomic energy.

During the remainder of the Truman administration the United States continued to press these proposals in the United Nations and elsewhere. Though the great majority of the countries accepted the basic principles of the plan, the Soviet Union, unfortunately, did not.

President Eisenhower was in office less than 3 months when he renewed the U.S. offer for "international control of atomic energy to promote its use for peaceful purposes only and to insure the prohibition of atomic weapons."

Two years later at the summit meeting in Geneva he personally launched the "open skies" proposal. Throughout the ensuing years, no matter what the temperature of the cold war, the United States has pursued in every available forum its search for peace through effective and verified disarmament.

These efforts disclosed a wide gap between the approach of this country and that of the Soviet Union to disarmament problems, mainly on the question of inspection and control. In the middle 1950's, therefore, the United States undertook to explore more limited measures.

The most promising of these was control of nuclear weapons testing. There were good reasons for this. All mankind had what might even be described as an instinctive impulse to end the pollution of the air and earth that was a consequence of unrestricted testing.

And, while arrangements banning bomb tests could not be wholly self-enforcing, the problem of detection and control seemed manageable. An agreement to stop testing — or not to begin — would not strip a nation of its defenses or carry it too far into the unknown. Here, many felt, was a good point from which to start.

The first Western proposal for control of nuclear tests was submitted to the Disarmament Subcommittee of the United Nations General Assembly on August 21, 1957. Sponsored by the United States, the United Kingdom, Canada, and France it called for a comprehensive 12-month ban on testing.

This proposal, however, again encountered the reluctance of Communist States, with closed societies, to accept the international inspection and control required for effective enforcement of a comprehensive ban. On April 13, 1959, after months of inconclusive debate on this issue of inspection and control, President Eisenhower and Prime Minister Macmillan advanced a proposal for a ban on tests in the atmosphere up to an altitude of 50 kilometers. This proposal did not require on-site inspection since significant tests of this kind could be detected and identified by national systems. Even this, however, was not accepted by the Soviet Union.

When the present administration assumed office, President Kennedy immediately undertook further explorations of the possibility of banning nuclear weapons tests. In 1961, President Kennedy, again with Prime Minister Macmillan, proposed a ban on tests in the atmosphere that would produce radioactive fallout. It was rejected by the U.S.S.R. The full text of a treaty embodying a ban on nuclear tests in the atmosphere, in outer space, and underwater, was tabled by the United States and United Kingdom delegations at Geneva on August 27, 1962.

At the same time, they tabled the text of a comprehensive treaty which provided for on-site inspections for detecting and identifying underground tests.

Before these texts were tabled there were consultations both with appropriate committees of Congress and with our allies and associates. For the past year, the text of a three-environment test ban has been before the world for comment and discussions. The treaty we have just signed in Moscow and which is now before you is based in its essential elements on the draft tabled in Geneva a year ago. Throughout this period, the concept has remained the same — to take a first step toward the control of nuclear weapons by prohibiting testing in those environments where our national systems are capable of detecting significant violations, leaving for subsequent steps the elimination of those tests that can be detected and identified only with an adequate system of inspection.

REASON FOR CONCERN WITH DISARMAMENT

Some may ask why three administrations representing both of our great political parties have devoted so much effort in attempting to make progress toward disarmament and, in particular, toward a ban on nuclear tests, when those same administrations were also building a nuclear arsenal of increasing and massive destructive power. The answer lies at the heart of the dilemma which troubles our world.

The values that are the heritage of a free society have been menaced by a Communist bloc armed with the most modern weapons and intent on world domination.

For our Nation this poses a special problem. We must, for our own security and as the leader of the free world, maintain a mastery of the most advanced weapons while technology moves forward at a breathtaking pace.

At the same time, we must use all our resources of will and intellect in an effort to halt the burdensome and dangerous competition in weapons that is the somber characteristic of the present world situation.

I recall the comment of a fellow officer in 1945 when we heard about the explosion of the first atom bomb. "War," he said, "has devoured itself."

Today the United States has operational weapons in its arsenal hundreds of times as destructive as that first atom bomb. The Polaris and Minuteman missiles are armed with warheads tens of times as powerful. The Soviets also have weapons of great destructive power.

The hard fact is that a full-scale nuclear exchange could erase all that man has built over the centuries. War has devoured itself because it can devour the world.

If our Nation is to survive today, we must be able at all times in the absence of the far-reaching disarmament which still eludes us to endure a nuclear attack and deliver counterblows of vast devastation. As Secretary McNamara will make clear tomorrow, we have the ability to do so. We intend to keep it that way, lest others be tempted by ambition to abandon reason.

Yet the facts must be faced. No one can realistically think of victory in a full-scale nuclear exchange. Last October during the Cuban crisis, men confronted decisions that might have moved to a nuclear war. That experience has been sobering for all.

No responsible man will deny that we live in a world of vast and incalculable risks. Where decisions may be required in minutes, we must be constantly on guard against the accident or miscalculation that can lead where no one wants to go. A local conflict anywhere around the globe in which the interests of the great powers are engaged might suddenly pose the prospect of nuclear war.

Nor can any responsible person say that we can improve our security by an unlimited arms race extending without relief into the future. On the contrary, great as the risks now are, they would rapidly increase. Arsenals will grow larger, weapons more destructive, the frustrations of stalemate and fear more intense. The risks will increase unpredictably as nuclear weapons become available to more and more countries.

It is against this prospect, which the world must frankly face, that the Senate is asked to consider the present treaty. If there may be marginal risks in it, they are far less in my opinion than the risks that will result if we accept the thought that rational man must pursue an unlimited competition in nuclear weapons.

All three of our Presidents who have borne supreme responsibility for our national security during the nuclear age have found the risks of an unlimited nuclear race far greater than those inherent in safe-guarded progress toward arms control.

Let me review with you the provisions of this treaty.

The treaty before you is a self-contained document and it embodies the whole of the agreement. As the President said in his message of transmittal, there are no side arrangements, understandings, or conditions of any kind.

EXPLANATION OF ARTICLE I

The fundamental obligation is set forth in article I. That article prohibits nuclear weapon tests as well as all other nuclear explosions in peacetime in three environments: the atmosphere, underwater, and outer space. Underground explosions are permitted so long as the radioactive debris remains within the country where the explosion takes place. Each party also undertakes not to assist any other country, whether or not a party, in conducting nuclear explosions of a kind prohibited under the treaty.

This treaty does not affect the use of nuclear weapons in war. It has to do with nuclear weapon testing in time of peace.

Nuclear explosions for peaceful purposes are, however, subject to the same limitations as nuclear weapons tests. This restriction is necessary because it is difficult to distinguish between the two without on-site inspection. It will not mean the end of our Plowshare program. Many of the peaceful experiments and uses in which we are interested can be conducted underground within the limits of the treaty. Dr. Seaborg will discuss this with you in detail.

ARTICLE II

Article II provides a procedure for amending the treaty. Amendments may be proposed by any party and are approved by a majority vote. The majority must include the United States, the United Kingdom, and the U.S.S.R. Amendments do not enter into force until instruments of ratification have been deposited by a majority of the parties, "including the instruments of ratification of all the original parties."

Thus, no amendment to the treaty can enter into force until it has been considered and approved by the Senate.

It has been said that this amendment process involves a veto. It does. I regard such a veto as essential to the security interests of the United States. Without it, the ban could be extended on terms and conditions that would be unacceptable — as, for example, to underground testing without on-site inspection.

Article II also provides that, if one-third of the parties so desires, a conference may be called to consider amendments, but a conference is not a necessary part of the amending process.

ARTICLE III

Article III prescribes the procedures for ratification and accession. We hope the treaty will have the widest possible application.

It has been suggested that, by the act of subscribing to the treaty, a regime might gain recognition by parties to the treaty that do not now recognize it. No such effect can occur. In international law the governing criterion of recognition is intent. We do not recognize, and we do not intend to recognize, the Soviet occupation zone of East Germany as a state or as an entity possessing national sovereignty, or to recognize the local authorities as a government. These authorities cannot alter these facts by the act of subscribing to the test ban treaty. The President made this clear in his press conference of August 1.

On August 2 the Department of State issued a formal statement to the same effect. Copies of both, Mr. Chairman, could appropriately be made a part of the record of this hearing.

The Chairman: They can be made so.

*   *   *   *   *

Secretary Rusk: All this would necessarily follow from the general rule of international law that participation in a multilateral treaty does not affect the recognition status of any authority or regime. But this treaty contains additional safeguards. Treaties typically provide for a single depositary. Article III, however, provides that each of the three original parties will be a depositary of the treaty. No depositary need accept a signature or an instrument of accession from authorities in a territory it does not recognize as a state.

The East German authorities will subscribe to the treaty in Moscow. The Soviet Union may notify us of that act. We are under no obligation to accept that notification, and we have no intention of doing so, but the East German regime would have committed itself to abide by the provisions of the treaty.

By this arrangement, we not only assure that no implication of recognition may arise, but we preserve our right to object if later the East German regime should seek to assert privileges under the treaty such as voting or participating in a conference called under article II.

ARTICLE IV

Article IV gives any party the right to withdraw from the treaty — "if it decides that extraordinary events, related to the subject matter of this treaty, have jeopardized the supreme interests of its country." A party must give 3 months' notice of its decision to withdraw. This provision is in our interest. If and when events occur that make testing in any of the three environments necessary for the security of the United States, we will be able to resume. Under the treaty, we alone will decide whether extraordinary events have occurred and whether they jeopardize our supreme national interests.

We need answer to no tribunal and to no authority other than our own conscience and requirements. We hope that the treaty will last and will grow in strength, but certainly no President of the United States would hesitate to exercise the right of withdrawal if the national security interest requires it.

If the Soviet Union itself were to test in violation of the treaty, the fundamental obligation that is the consideration for our adherence would disappear. In that case, the United States could, if it chose, consider itself released from its reciprocal obligation and could resume testing without delay.

MAINTENANCE OF NATIONAL SECURITY

Under this treaty, the national security of the United States can and will be fully maintained.

This country has learned much from the experience of the last 18 years. We do not propose to forget those lessons. We have no basis yet for assuming a fundamental change in Soviet objectives. We are still engaged in a contest between free choice and coercion. The President made this clear, and I want to reiterate it here today.

But there is nothing inconsistent between this treaty, or other effectively enforceable arms control agreements, and a policy of vigilance. The same three administrations that have sought disarmament over the past 18 years have effectively met Communist threats of aggression — in Iran, in Greece and Turkey, in Berlin and Western Europe, in Korea, in southeast Asia, in Cuba. But whatever may be the fundamental antagonisms between us and the Soviet Union, we have a mutual interest in avoiding mutual destruction.

We shall remain ready to meet further challenges. The treaty permits underground testing. The policy of the United States is to continue to test underground as necessary to our security. Moreover, although we hope for compliance, we cannot discount the possibility that the Soviet Union may violate the treaty. We shall be on the alert for any violations, and we have a high degree of confidence in our ability to detect them. The Secretary of Defense and the Director of the Central Intelligence Agency will discuss this capability in detail. But I am confident that, if significant testing in violation of the treaty takes place, we will know about it. And we will be ready at all times to resume testing in all environments, and promptly, if that should become necessary. Dr. Seaborg will be prepared to deal with these matters in considerable detail.

Concrete Gains from Treaty

This is a limited treaty. The President listed the things it does not do, and we must keep them in mind in judging its significance. At the same time, if — as seems likely — most of the nations of the world adhere to the treaty, and if they observe its obligations, this will in itself bring concrete gains.

First, the United States and the Soviet Union already have enough nuclear power to inflict enormous destruction on each other. Still, the search for bigger, more destructive weapons goes on. Each generation of major weapons has been more expensive than the last. Each has involved an increasing burden, an increasing diversion of resources from the great unfinished business of mankind. Yet greater armament has not demonstrably brought greater security. The treaty, if observed, should slow this spiral, without damage to our relative strength.

Second, the treaty will help contain the spread of nuclear weapons. We cannot guarantee it. Most of the countries with the capacity and the incentive to develop nuclear weapons over the next decade or so have already announced that they will accept the self-denying ordinance of the treaty. These countries do not include, by the way, mainland China or France.

While this does not guarantee that they will never become nuclear powers, their renunciation of atmospheric testing will act as a deterrent by making it much more difficult and expensive for them to develop nuclear weapons.

Third, the treaty will reduce the radioactive pollution of the planet. The increased radioactivity from nuclear testing has thus far stayed within tolerable limits, in a statistical sense. But as the President said: "This is not a natural hazard, and it is not a statistical issue."

Moreover, if testing were not restricted, more and more countries would conduct tests. Many of them would lack either the incentive or the means to minimize the fallout. We have a high obligation to safeguard life and health and the genetic integrity of the human race. Today no one can say for certain how much fallout is too much. But if this treaty is observed it will go a long way to assure that we do not transgress those limits.

OPENING OF NEW PATHS

For 18 years we have held the Communist drive in check largely by the deterrent force of our massive military strength. We shall maintain that overwhelming strength until we are certain that freedom can be assured by other means.

But throughout we have known that a lasting peace could not be founded upon armed might alone. It can be secured only by durable international institutions, and by a respect for law and its procedures.

The problem has been to convince the Communist world that its interest also lay in that direction.

The most important thing about the treaty is, therefore, what it may symbolize and what new paths it may open. That, no one can now foretell.

But as the Senate undertakes its appraisal of this treaty it is well to recall the vivid statement that Bernard Baruch made to the United Nations when the nuclear age was first upon us: "We are here" — he said — "to make a choice between the quick and the dead. . . .

"Behind the black portent of the new atomic age lies a hope which, seized upon with faith, can work our salvation. If we fail, then we have damned every man to be the slave of fear."

For 17 years all men have lived in that shadow of that fear. But if the promise of this treaty can be realized, if we can now take even this one small step along a new course, then frail and fearful mankind may find another step and another until confidence replaces terror and hope takes over from despair.

Thank you very much, Mr. Chairman.

An Eminent Scientist Questions the Test Ban Treaty

EDWARD TELLER

Dr. Teller: The President of the United States has asked for a full discussion of the test ban treaty, this most important treaty, which is before you.

WORRY OVER TREATY

Those of us who are worried about this treaty have a clear and strong obligation to put before you our worries. I intend to do this, and I intend to try and do it with complete frankness, and with the proper kind of moderation which the importance of the occasion demands.

I have already told you that I am worried about the treaty, and I want to make it clear at the very outset what the basis of this worry is in general terms.

The purpose of the treaty is to safeguard peace, to make a step toward peace. There cannot be and there is not any difference of opinion on this basic point. Peace has been of the greatest importance at all times, but today when I know very well how sudden and how devastating war can be, peace is more important than it has been ever before.

Statement of Edward Teller, University of California, *Nuclear Test Ban Treaty*, Hearings before the Committee on Foreign Relations, United States Senate, 88th Congress, 1st Session, U.S. Government Printing Office, Washington, D.C., 1963, pp. 417–28.

TREATY — POSSIBLY A STEP TO WAR

The reason that I am worried about this treaty is because I believe that this treaty is a step not toward peace but rather a step away from safety, possibly a step toward war.

In January, it will be 25 years that I have heard, together with quite a few other scientists, at a conference which we organized here in Washington, about nuclear fission. Within a few days the grave consequences of this discovery have become clear to most of us. This worry has not left me in this past quarter of a century. I want to start out by telling you something about this long period, and by emphasizing one particular point.

CONSTANT NUCLEAR SURPRISES

This time has been a time of extremely rapid development, and it has been a time full of surprises. At no turn did we know what the next step will bring. At no time could most of us predict the future. Yet what we are now trying to do is essentially to attempt to predict the future, and when some of the best and most outstanding people contradict each other, they do so because the future is necessarily uncertain.

I beg you to have patience with me, to tell you a little of the past in order to put the future into perspective.

During the war many of us have labored diligently and with success on the first nuclear explosion. Even then the result was a surprise. You may not know it but at the day when the first nuclear explosive was fired no serious prediction succeeded in guessing at the real size of the explosion.

All of us have underestimated it.

After 4 years of strenuous effort, of theoretical calculations, of careful design, we did not succeed to predict what is going to happen. We succeeded in making something that was effective but experiment could not have been replaced by any prediction.

Right after the explosion, shortly after, the director of the laboratory made a statement to me which I will never forget. He said, "We have done an excellent job, and very many years will pass before anybody will be able to improve it in any important detail."

This is an old story now and the point is gone. You know that only 6 years later another step was taken. That step was taken under the stimulus of another surprise. Most of us believed and the U.S. intelligence firmly and unequivocally predicted, that the Russians will not have a nuclear explosion for many years.

The first Russian test in 1949 was a complete surprise. Some of us got worried. I got very worried about the next surprise that might be in store for us, and we started out on the next step which the majority of the scientists said could not be done, the thermonuclear explosion.

You know that within a short time that succeeded, with an effect almost a thousand times as great as the first explosion, and that, in turn, was followed within a few months with the Russians producing something that looked very much like a thermonuclear explosion.

Again, in contradiction to all expectations, to all predictions, to the explicit statements of the intelligence community.

In time these big explosions have triggered another development in the United States, the development of missiles.

Right after the war the judgment was that accuracy of these missiles cannot be great enough to justify carrying the relatively small nuclear explosives available at that time.

With the thermonuclear explosives there was no more any possibility to avoid the knowledge. Missiles, very important, could have a deadly significance. Yet while we were getting started on missiles, while General Shriver, who I understand is testifying today, has done the most excellent and the most fantastic job in developing our own missile systems, we still did not realize the great potentialities that rockets would have in space exploration, and 1957 Sputnik took us by surprise once again.

Intelligence did not alert our Government about that important step, and we went into the missile age with deficient preparation.

TEST RESULTS IN 1958

During our last big well-planned test series in 1958, the missile age was still young, and the experiments which we then performed did not have as much a relation to our preparation for the missile age as they should have.

Let me explain this. We had succeeded in making big explosions. We had succeeded in making these big explosives light, and while we succeeded we know we can develop further, but I do not claim that the further developments will be of very great additional significance. There is another point which we have neglected.

In 1958 none of us believed in any serious way that missile defense is a realistic possibility. We have not studied the effects or not studied most of the effects which are of primary importance in trying to stop a missile, and which are of great importance in defending our own missile sites which at that time hardly existed, against the attack of incoming missiles.

You all know that in 1958 we went into a prolonged moratorium and here again even during the moratorium while we tried hard to foresee what is going to happen, we did not foresee.

In some little respect we succeeded to make an extremely important step.

Underground Tests in 1957

In 1957 we made our first underground nuclear explosion. It was a small one. I argued long for it and strongly, mostly on the basis that this is an unknown area which we should explore. We explored it in the scientific field, we learned a lot from it, and we learned something else, that we did not really expect to learn. We learned something about the possibility of clandestine testing. This was not in my mind when I proposed the 1957 explosion, but when we sat down to the conference table in 1958, as the months went by, it became clearer and clearer that big atmospheric explosions can be policed, that there is real doubt about small atmospheric explosions, and that there is most serious doubt about explosions underground, and also in space. That underground explosions cannot be policed, that this point had to be taken seriously because known to us only because of the accident that for other reasons — for reasons of scientific curiosity — we happened to make a test of an underground explosion in 1957.

How important this fact has become later, I don't need to tell you.

Russian Tests Resumed — 1961

You all know what the next surprise is, because surprises in the past are not surprising. In the summer of 1961 the Russians resumed testing, in the late summer.

We know now that this test series was by far the most powerful, we have reason to believe that it was the most powerful in the whole history of Russian preparations, and it was the most plentiful, the most repetitious, the most solid ever carried out by any nation.

I don't think that any expert will disagree with me when I say that this test series had to be prepared for many months in advance, and that the preparations had to be expensive, widespread, and should have been open to intelligence information. It is possible, I would even say that it is probable that the planning of this abrogation took a time longer than a year.

Yet on the day before Khrushchev made his announcement our Government still did not know that a test series was impending.

Here is another surprise, another failure of us to predict what the future will bring and what the Russians intend to do.

RUSSIAN ADVANCES — RESULT OF TESTING

As a result of this test series the Russians made a big explosion. For one I can tell you this was no surprise. I wish I could talk about it more. It is interesting, it is slightly relevant, it is classified, but the Russians did have a surprise in store for us, and that surprise was their announcement and evidence supporting that announcement that they did make great strides toward missile defense.

In 1961, and in the similarly impressive test series in 1962, the Russians had every chance in the world to make the observations in the atmosphere which are the firm basis of any plan for an effective or halfway effective missile defense, and I am saying halfway effective in the most serious way.

MISSILE DEFENSE POSSIBLE

A few years ago I firmly believed that missile defense was hopeless. I am now convinced that I was wrong. Stimulated by the Russian statements, we have looked into the matter very thoroughly and I now believe, I am now convinced that we can put up a missile defense that can stop the attack of any weaker power such as China, for the next two decades.

In a time when we rightly worry about proliferation we must not neglect our defenses against an attack from a quarter other than Russia. In addition I also believe that our defense can be partially effective against the Russians. We may not be able to save our cities, we may be able to save our retaliatory capacity, and thereby we may lend force to the argument that we can hit back and that the Russians, therefore, will not hit first.

We can make a missile defense, in all probability, that will safeguard at least reasonably strongly built shelters which one can build in great numbers and which we should build.

No matter what we do in missile defense, I still believe that the nuclear war will be very terrible, but missile defense may make the difference between the end of our national existence and our survival as a nation.

And, perhaps even more important, missile defense, by deterring the Russians, may make the difference between peace and war.

Excuse me, that I have made this introduction. As you will see, what I have said is relevant in several respects. I have now arrived at the point of the present test treaty. This test treaty is to be viewed in our past experience. I will try to be brief. I hope that the many and complex questions connected with this treaty will be brought out by your questions. I want to concentrate on the main argument for the treaty, and on the main argument against the treaty.

These arguments are extremely important, and I would not like to obscure the issue by trying to give you a bag full of arguments — some important, some not.

Argument For

The argument, the strongest argument, in my mind, for the treaty is to stop the spread of nuclear weapons. We have been worried about such a spread for many years, and rightfully so.

We know, today, that it is easy to make nuclear explosions, and that any country that can acquire nuclear materials can make an explosion within a year. Yet it has been claimed that this treaty will stop proliferation. Why?

Underground Testing Expensive

Secretary Rusk and Secretary McNamara, in their testimony, have spelled out the answer very simply and very clearly. Any nation which signs this treaty will have to test, if it tests at all, underground, and underground testing is more expensive.

On this point, however, there is a simple statement I can make, a simple statement connected with dollars about which there is no doubt. An underground test of a magnitude that has been traditional for the first test of any nation, will cost approximately a million dollars. This cost, I want to make very clear, is the cost of testing. It does not include the cost of the weapon. It certainly does not include the much bigger cost of the whole development of nuclear reactors or whatever else had to be done to make the material, of the research that went into putting the material together.

This million dollar figure that I mentioned to you is, I think, slightly higher, not very much higher, than the cost that would be incurred if the test were performed in the atmosphere. But no matter how these two costs compare, once a nation has gone to the expense of developing a nuclear explosive, the additional single million dollars that is needed for underground testing will certainly not be a financial deterrent.

I had an opportunity, a few days ago, to make the statement to Secretary McNamara. He answered that he did not mean the cost in dollars. He meant the psychological and political cost.

I am not an expert in psychological and political costs. I am glad to concede that, under this test treaty, the Swedes and the Swiss may refrain from underground testing in order to be as completely in agreement with world opinion as they can be. I doubt whether more dangerous nations will be so deterred.

This, as far as I can see, is the argument, and the only argument, against proliferation.

Argument Against

Let me now turn to the main argument against the treaty. This treaty will permit the Russians and us, and anybody else, to develop nuclear explosives underground. This will permit us to perfect not every kind of an aggressive weapon, but very important kinds of aggressive weapons. This treaty, therefore, will not have the direct effect of slowing down the development of aggressive weapons. What it will do is to prohibit us from acquiring the knowledge about effects of weapons, those effects which are of vital importance in ballistic missile defense.

In the early 1950's, we made plenty of observations on the effects of nuclear explosives on houses, on ships. But in those days we were not talking about missile silos. In those days, we did not investigate the way how nuclear explosives can be used. We did not investigate the way how nuclear explosives can be used to stop a missile attack.

The 1962 U.S. Tests Showed Need for More

In the missile age, we have performed only one test series in the atmosphere in 1962. This we have performed with little planning, in a great hurry, and I would like to state that we ended with the conviction that the amount of knowledge that we still desperately need vastly exceeds the knowledge that we already possess. In the same missile age the Russians have tested in an essentially unrestricted manner.

Secretary McNamara has told you that on missile defense the Russians have probably no more information than we do. How does he know? There are some experiments which are unmistakably designed for missile defense. These are few, but, in very many other experiments, apparatus may have been around, probably was around, that looked at effects relevant to missile defense.

Limited Information re U.S.S.R. Nuclear Knowledge

Our information about nuclear explosions in Russia is very limited. What we know firmly is only the great extent of our ignorance. What, in these more than 100 atmospheric explosions, the Russians may have learned about atmospheric tests, about missile defense, we have no better way of knowing than we had a way of knowing whether they prepared a test series in 1961.

On the basis of the past performance of our intelligence, we cannot be comfortable and we cannot say that we know what the Russians know. What we must say is that they had 3 or perhaps 4 times more opportunity to find out the relevant facts on missile defense than we had.

I am going to continue to talk to you for a short time about this question of missile defense, and I will do it by referring to a connected important topic.

Secretary McNamara has told you that we are stronger than the Russians, that we have many more missiles, that when they build more missiles we will know it, and we will outbuild them any time.

Perhaps our intelligence has now improved sufficiently that we can rely upon it. I hope so, although I must also say that of all things where it is difficult to compete with a police state, intelligence is likely to be the most difficult.

U.S.S.R. Has Knowledge re Missile Defense

But this test ban has nothing at all to do with how many missiles either side builds. This test ban has something to do with knowledge, and it does not have to do so much with knowledge concerning aggressive potentials. It has something vitally important to do with knowledge concerning missile defense, concerning the vulnerability of our retaliatory forces. I believe that the Russians have acquired this knowledge. I believe that, because they have acquired this knowledge, they don't need any more atmospheric tests, and I believe that is why Khrushchev is willing to sign the treaty at present.

In 1960, he wasn't willing to sign, but now he had these magnificent test series of 1961 and 1962. He now knows how to defend himself. He now knows, probably, where the weaknesses lie in our defense. He has the knowledge, and he is now willing to stop and prevent us from obtaining similar knowledge.

If the Russians want to build a big missile force with which to attack us, they can do so legally under the present testing. What they need is knowledge, and that is what they have. What we need is knowledge and that is what we don't have.

EFFECT OF TREATY ON ARMS RACE

Secretary McNamara has told you that if you don't have enough knowledge about the hardening of our missile sites we will make up for it by building more missiles, by spacing these missiles farther apart, by making them harder. All this costs money. All this costs billions of dollars. What Secretary McNamara is telling you is that he is willing to substitute brawn for brain, and to spend more and more money for defense. This is what has been rightly called an arms race. To acquire more knowledge, to acquire more knowledge in order to know how to defend ourselves, this, I would suggest, is not quite properly called an arms race.

This treaty will not prevent the arms race. It will stimulate it. This treaty is not directed against the arms race. This treaty is directed against knowledge, our knowledge.

Why do we need this knowledge?

LIMITS ON KNOWLEDGE GAINED BY UNITED STATES UNDER A TREATY

Secretary McNamara has told you, and he is right, that we can do a lot about missile defense. We can study the incoming missiles, we can study the decoys, and we can try to see the difference between them. We can perfect our radars, make them harder, more versatile, faster.

By underground testing we can develop the best kind of nuclear explosives by which to kill an incoming missile, because when you are shooting at such a fast and uncertain target as an incoming missile, you cannot hit it with a bull's-eye. You need a powerful counterforce, a small nuclear explosion.

Secretary McNamara has said rightly that we can do all that.

But there is one thing, one circumstance he did not explain. He did not explain to you that we must expect not 1 missile to come against us, but 5, and not to come alone but to come accompanied by 25 decoys. We have to discriminate between these, find out which are the dangerous objects and shoot them down, not some of them but all of them. The first shot that we fire will blind us, and will make us less prepared to shoot against the second missile that comes hard on the heels of the first.

Missile Defense Needs Complex Experiments

To do that is easy. It is very easy for a powerful country like the Soviet Union. That there is this difficulty we know. How big the difficulty, how to circumvent it, what to do about it, needs experimentation and more experimentation. Missile defense is the most complex military operation that I have ever been in touch with. To try to build up our missile defense forces without proper and complete experimentation, experimentation that can be performed faithfully and in a relevant way only in the atmosphere, to do without this experimentation is most hazardous.

Sokolovsky's Military Strategy

No underground tests can take the place of the actual tryout.

The Russians had an opportunity. They had also a motive. Some of you may have read, all of you will have heard, of the recent book by Marshal Sokolovsky; he did not actually write it, that has been translated from the Russian and is now available to us. The title of the book is "Military Strategy." And if you read that book you cannot be left in doubt about the great importance that the Russians, who had been hurt so badly at the beginning of the First World War — of the Second World War, the great importance that they place upon air defense and missile defense.

We are still hesitating whether to put in a missile defense. The Russians are working on it. With all the uncertainty that will continue to be with us in this test ban, we may never put in our missile defense.

This test ban has given the Russians the knowledge on the basis of which they can now proceed and spend money in a reasonable way. We do not have the corresponding knowledge.

WEAKENED DEFENSES A RESULT OF TREATY

This is the main argument against the test ban treaty. It weakens our defense, and as long as we have reason to distrust Soviet intentions, the weakness of our defense will invite attack.

This is why I say that this treaty is a step, not more than a step, but a step, in the wrong direction.

There are some additional points. Will we know, as Secretary McNamara has said, when the Russians begin to deploy more missiles, more radar. I certainly hope so. I believe it but I do not believe it with complete assurance, not after the many disappointments we had in predicting what the Russians will do. There is an additional way of no less importance. We should and we may deploy a missile defense which might not be as good as it could be if we had more knowledge, but which might be satisfactory anyway. The best we can do, perhaps enough to deter the Russian aggression. But will we help our allies, will we give as we should give to our allies defensive missiles, thousands of them, as we should?

MISSILES TO ALLIES FOR DEFENSE

If we don't, if we defend ourselves, and leave our allies undefended, our allies who are closer to Russia, who are menaced by the cheaper and more numerous intermediate range missiles, if we do that, I think it will be a clear and strong psychological force that will drive the alliance apart.

But I am sure you are raising the question in your minds: Could we, would we, in any case, give these missiles to our allies giving them thousands of nuclear warheads, would that not have the same effect as proliferation?

Would it not invite war by accident? Would it not risk misuse? I am saying to you that we can do it without any of these risks. We can tie missiles to their sites, nuclear warheads to the missiles. We can put into the whole system an electronic program such that the missile will not explode before it has reached an altitude where it can do no damage on the ground. We can make sure that the missile will explode or otherwise be destroyed before it leaves the territory of the country that had fired the missile. These missiles cannot be used for anything except to shoot down flying objects. It can be used for only one purpose, for a justified self-defense.

I believe that at least in the spirit of our present laws, we could do this, and I think we should do this if we ever get a reasonably satisfactory missile defense, and this is the way how together with our allies, with common work and common results we could strengthen our alliance.

TREATY EFFECT ON NUCLEAR SHARING

But, as far as I read the text of this treaty, this treaty prevents any such measure. The treaty says that we must not help, aid, encourage, or in any way participate in somebody else's nuclear test explosion or in any other nuclear explosion carried out by somebody else.

If we give the Belgians a defensive missile, and a button to push, and they only have to push the button and the missile goes off and explodes over Belgium harmlessly, if we make sure, as we must make sure that they can push the button in self-defense any time without calling Washington, because these missiles are flying only for minutes and if the emergency arises you must push the button and make no phone calls.

If we do that, have we not aided, encouraged, and participated in potential explosion?

If the Russians would claim to have installed such defensive missiles in Cuba, would we take it?

IS TREATY A BARRIER BETWEEN ALLIES?

We have no other possibility in order to save our alliance, to make the defenses common. Yet to me it seems that this treaty, unless very thoroughly amended, will erect a big barrier between our allies and ourselves in a most important area of defense.

I could add that the treaty calls into question our ability to come to the aid of a country in Asia in case this country could be invaded.

What if the Chinese march over the Himalayan passes and we have reason to believe that India will be conquered in 6 weeks long before we had time to send over men and supplies. We still could close the Himalayan passes by nuclear explosives. But the treaty says we must not perform a nuclear test explosion or any other nuclear explosion.

I know very well that Secretary Rusk has stated that in case of war we can use these explosions. Still I am uneasy. I do not know what the precise legal situation is, and I know that even if legally the treaty says the opposite of what it appears to say, the psychological impact will be enormous, and the treaty will perhaps even rightly hold our hand if we try to help in the defense of freedom anywhere on the globe.

More than that, other nations reading this treaty will question our will to support them if the case should seriously arise.

I certainly would have wished that if this treaty had to be drafted it should have excluded nuclear test explosions and not any other explosions. We must maintain our right to use nuclear explosions in our defense, in the defense of our allies, and in the defense of any country against massive aggression.

FUTURE PEACEFUL DEVELOPMENTS

I have talked about the past, and I have talked about the present. I would like to say a few words about the future. There is another surprise around the corner, and the surprise is not so great because some of us have foreseen it, and worked for it for years.

When it comes the surprise still will be great, because people barely begin to believe us. During this very year of 1963 we claim, and we are convinced that we can use nuclear explosions for peaceful purposes. We can move great amounts of earth for one-tenth the amount of money that it used to cost us to move earth.

We can make harbors, we can make sea level canals, we can deflect rivers, we can throw off overburden from deep deposits, deep mineral deposits and increase our wealth and the wealth of other nations. We can do it in a very clean way. We can do it in such a way, I believe, 2 years from now it will be possible to make an explosion that will have made a crater and land in this crater as soon as the dust has settled, in 15 minutes, without exposing ourselves to more radiation than we have taken year in and year out in our laboratories. All this can be done. But there will be some measurable radioactivity, and this treaty prohibits the deposition of any radioactivity outside the territory of the United States.

PROBLEMS OF PEACEFUL DEVELOPMENT UNDER TREATY

Can we build a sea level canal? Can we help a backward country in making a harbor or getting at its mineral deposits? Can we do so legally by a simple agreement between us and that country or do we have to go for permission from case to case to the Soviet Union?

The Chairman of the Atomic Energy Commission, Glenn Seaborg, has rightly emphasized the great importance of Plowshare. He has rightly stated that the treaty does not prohibit our developing Plowshare inside the United States as long as no radioactivity is deposited elsewhere, and he also said that when we have fully developed this capability then we will go back to the Russians and ask for a change in the treaty.

I hope, and I am not completely convinced, that the Russians will observe the treaty, and will not break it in a clandestine way. I certainly am a little doubtful whether the Russians will be willing to change the treaty in the future in order to please us, whether they will be willing to give up a hold that this treaty gives them over our negotiations with friends and other countries.

The treaty explicitly prohibits nuclear explosions in space; yet many of the possible futuristic and as yet unproven applications of Plowshare, of the peaceful uses, lie in space exploration.

Treaty's Effect on Knowledge

Even space propulsion may become possible using nuclear explosions. This treaty is a treaty whose main point is to bar knowledge, to prohibit knowledge, the acquiring of knowledge that we need now for our defense and it also interferes with knowledge which we may acquire otherwise in the future, and which we may want for scientific purposes, for the purpose of a big and expensive space adventure.

Summary

I am at the end of my statement. I want to summarize. I know that this treaty has been signed by now by more than 60 nations. I know that it will be a very difficult thing not to ratify it. Because of the terrific setback this will give to American diplomacy, I am prepared to say, although this is not my field, that it would be a mistake not to ratify the treaty.

Senator Pastore: Would you say that again, please?

Dr. Teller: I say that as an inexpert witness in diplomacy I am willing to admit that not to ratify the treaty would be a mistake. But I want to say that this treaty prohibits future science, future progress, the kind of thing on which the greatness of this country has been based.

I say that this treaty erects barriers between our allies and ourselves, and may lead to the disintegration of NATO, and I say that this treaty makes it very hard and very dubious whether we can defend our own country as well as we otherwise might defend it.

These, to my mind, are overriding considerations. I, therefore, say to have signed the treaty was a mistake. Having made this mistake, no matter what you do next will be a mistake. To ratify it will be a small mistake.

Senator Humphrey: Would you repeat that again, Doctor?

Dr. Teller: I am sorry, I didn't mean to say that. If you reject the treaty this will be a small mistake. It will be a painful mistake to reject the treaty but it will not endanger the future of the United States.

If you ratify this treaty I think you will have committed an enormously bigger mistake. You will have given away the future safety of this country. You will have increased the chances of war, and, therefore, no matter what the embarrassment may be in rejecting the treaty, I earnestly urge you to do so and not to ratify the treaty which is before you.

Thank you very much.

THE EXECUTIVE BRANCH

3   The Presidency

The Presidency is at once the most visible of our national institutions and the most obscure. Its visibility is obvious and needs no further word. It is precisely the ubiquity of the modern Presidency that has kept us from an awareness of many important aspects of the office that are not part of the common lore. We think we know what it must be like to be President; yet even Presidents themselves, when they have taken office, have been appalled at the newly revealed dimensions of the job. Our ignorance of this political office is due in no small part to the fact that it is generally inaccessible to the trained and systematic observer. In addition, if we date the modern Presidency to Franklin D. Roosevelt, only five men have occupied it. These men have had different styles and experiences, have behaved in different ways, and have confronted different orders of problems, all of which have made good and accurate generalizations about the modern Presidency difficult to come by.[1] Professor Neustadt, author of Presidential Power (*New York: John Wiley & Sons, Inc., 1960), is a trained observer who has been close to several of these Presidents. In the following statement, part of his testimony before the "Jackson Subcommittee," he writes not about the powers of the President but about his problems which grow out of a competitive-cooperative relationship with other officials in the Executive branch who exercise some of his formal powers.*

[1] See, in this connection, Nelson W. Polsby, *Congress and the Presidency* (Englewood Cliffs, N.J.: Prentice-Hall, Inc., 1964), esp. Chap. 2, "The Presidency."

The Presidency, the Executive Branch, and National Security

RICHARD E. NEUSTADT

Mr. Neustadt: Thank you, Mr. Chairman and Senator Javits. It is a privilege to appear before you. This subcommittee and its predecessor* have contributed a great deal to the fund of information on which we in universities depend for the enlightenment of those we teach. If I can be of use to you today, please take it with my thanks as a return for benefits received.

You have asked me to comment on basic issues in national security staffing and operations. This is a vast field and a very complex one, where troubles are hard to track down and "solutions" come harder still. The field is full of genuine dilemmas, many of them quite new to our governmental system but all of them quite likely to endure as far ahead as one can see. Durability is a common characteristic. So is difficulty.

Perhaps the chief of these dilemmas is the one placed first in the subcommittee's recent, cogent staff report on "Basic Issues." To quote from that report:

> The needs of a President and the needs of the departments and agencies are not identical. . . .
> What does a President need to do his job?
> Essentially . . . to keep control . . . to get early warning of items for his agenda before his options are foreclosed, to pick his issues and lift these out of normal channels, to obtain priority attention from key officials

Statement of Dr. Richard E. Neustadt, Professor of Government, Columbia University, *Administration of National Security*, Hearings before the Subcommittee on National Security Staffing and Operations of the Committee on Government Operations, United States Senate, 88th Congress, 1st Session, U.S. Government Printing Office, Washington, D.C., 1963, Part I, pp. 74–84.

* Subcommittee on National Policy Machinery of the Committee on Government Operations, U.S. Senate.

on the issues he pulls to his desk, to get prompt support for his initiatives, and to keep other matters on a smooth course, with his lines of information open, so that he can intervene if need arises. . . .

What do the officials of our vast departments and agencies need to do their jobs?

Essentially . . . orderly, deliberate, familiar procedures — accustomed forms in which to air their interests, a top-level umpire to blow the whistle . . . written records of the decisions by which they should be governed.

. . . [M]iddle-level yearnings for . . . [a coordinating mechanism originate] in the desire to have one's views heard through some set, certain, reliable procedure which binds the highest levels as well as other agencies.

A President needs flexibility, freedom to improvise, in dealing with those below. Officialdom needs stability, assurance of regularity, in dealing with those above. To a degree these needs are incompatible; hence the dilemma. As your staff report notes:

It is not surprising that the departments often find a President's way of doing business unsettling — or that Presidents sometimes view the departments almost as adversaries.

In considering the problems now before you, I find it the beginning of wisdom to face this dilemma candidly. That is what I hope to do today.

THE PRESIDENT VERSUS OFFICIALDOM

So much of our literature and everyday discussion treats the executive branch as though it were an entity that effort is required to visualize the President apart from the departments, in effect a separate "branch," with needs and interests differing from those of "his" officialdom. Yet constitutional prescription, political tradition, governmental practice, and democratic theory all unite to make this so. In all these terms the separateness of Presidential need and interest are inevitable — and legitimate.

The man in the White House is constitutional commander of our military forces, conductor of foreign relations, selector of department heads, custodian of the "take care clause" and of the veto power. No other person in our system has so massive a responsibility for national security. At the same time he is the one executive official holding office on popular election, and save for the Vice President he is our only public officer accountable directly to a national electorate. He is, besides, a relative short-timer in our Government. Members of Congress and career officials often hold high places for a generation. He, at most, holds his for just 8 years. The first year is a learning time, the last year usually a stalemate. Whatever personal imprint he can hope to make is usually reserved to the short span between. Yet his name becomes the label for an "era" in the history books; his accountability widens as time goes on. Schoolchildren yet unborn may hold him personally responsible for everything that happens to the country in "his" years.

The constitutional responsibility, the political accountability, the time perspective, the judgment of history: all these adhere to the President himself, not as an "institution" but as a human being. In this combination his situation is unique. No one else in the executive branch — or for that matter in the Government — shares equally in his responsibility or feels an equal heat from his electorate and history. It is no wonder that his needs can be distinguished from, and actually are different from, the needs of most officials in executive departments.

Cold war and nuclear weapons make the difference greater. A new dimension of risk has come upon American decision-making. Its effect has been to magnify the President's responsibility, and to intensify his needs for flexibility, for information, for control. This new dimension first began to manifest itself in President Eisenhower's second term. Mr. Kennedy is the first President to live with it from the outset of his administration.

THE PRESIDENT AS RISKTAKER

What a President now lives with is the consequence of a substantial nuclear delivery capability acquired by the Soviet Union as well as the United States. It is the mutual capability which pushes our decision-making — and theirs, too, of course — into a new dimension of risk. In an article included in your volume of selected papers, I have termed this the risk of "irreversibility," the risk that either bureaucratic momentum in a large-scale undertaking or mutual miscalculation by atomic adversaries, or both combined, may make it infeasible to call back, or play over, or revise, an action taken in our foreign relations, at least within the range of the cold war. But the term "irreversibility," standing alone, does not really suffice to convey what is new in this dimension. Bureaucratic momentum and multiple miscalculations made a German emperor's snap reaction after Sarajevo "irreversible" as long ago as July 1914. Therefore, to amend the term: What is new since the Soviets acquired their ICBM's is the risk of irreversibility become irremediable. Unlike the problems facing Kaiser Wilhelm 50 years ago — or those of President Roosevelt in World War II, or even those of President Truman in Korea — a possible result of present action is that nothing one does later can ward off, reduce, repair, or compensate for costs to one's society.

Let me underscore this point; it goes to the heart of my presentation today. Last October we all glimpsed the new dimension in a President's risktaking. But the Cuban confrontation seems to me a relatively simplified affair: geographically, in the issue raised, in the number of contestants, and in duration. What if there were two or three such issues simultaneously, or stretched over 2 months instead of 2 weeks? What if there were — as Mr. Kennedy told us last week there may be 10 years hence — a multiplicity of nuclear powers, a multiplicity of possible miscalculators, each capable of setting off irreparable consequences? Consider the next President's risktaking, let alone Mr. Kennedy's. This new dimension deepens year by year.

The consequences for the Presidency are profound.

One consequence is that the sitting President lives daily with the knowledge that at any time he, personally, may have to make a human judgment — or may fail to control someone else's judgment — which puts half the world in jeopardy and cannot be called back. You and I will recognize his burden intellectually; he actually experiences it emotionally. It cannot help but set him — and his needs — sharply apart from all the rest of us, not least from the officials who have only to advise him. As Mr. Kennedy remarked in his December television interview: "The President bears the burden of the responsibility. The advisers may move on to new advice."

A second related consequence is that now more than ever before his mind becomes the only source available from which to draw politically legitimated judgments on what, broadly speaking, can be termed the political feasibilities of contemplated action vis-à-vis our world antagonists: judgments on where history is tending, what opponents can stand, what friends will take, what officials will enforce, what "men in the street" will tolerate; judgments on the balance of support, opposition, indifference at home and abroad. Our Constitution contemplated that such judgments should emanate from President and Congress, from a combination of the men who owed their places to electorates, who had themselves experienced the hazards of nomination and election. The democratic element in our system consists, essentially, of reserving these judgments to men with that experience. But when it comes to action risking war, technology has modified the Constitution: the President, perforce, becomes the only such man in the system capable of exercising judgment under the extraordinary limits now imposed by secrecy, complexity, and time.

Therefore as a matter not alone of securing his own peace of mind, but also of preserving the essentials in our democratic order, a President, these days, is virtually compelled to reach for information and to seek control over details of operation deep inside executive departments. For it is at the level of detail, of concrete plans, of actual performance, on "small" operations, to say nothing of large ones, that there often is a fleeting chance — sometimes the only chance — to interject effective judgment. And it is at this level that risks of the gravest sort are often run. "Irreversibility becomes irremediable" is not to be considered something separate from details of operation. If, as reported, Mr. Kennedy kept track of every movement of blockading warships during the Cuban crisis of October 1962, this is but a natural and necessary corollary of the new dimension of risk shadowing us all, but most of all a President.

The net effect is to restrict, if not repeal, a hallowed aspect of American military doctrine, the autonomy of field commanders, which as recently as Mr. Truman's time, as recently as the Korean war, was thought to set sharp limits upon White House intervention in details of operation. The conduct of diplomacy is comparably affected. So, I presume, is the conduct of intelligence. Also, we now rediscover that age-old problem for the rulers of States: timely and secure communications. The complications here are mind stretching.

The only persons qualified to give you a full appreciation of the President's felt needs in such a situation are Mr. Eisenhower, keeping his last years in view, and Mr. Kennedy. Mr. Khrushchev might now be equipped to offer some contributory evidence. The situation is so new and so unprecedented that outside the narrow circle of these men and their immediate associates one cannot look with confidence for understanding of their prospects or requirements as these appear to them. I do not advance this caution out of modesty — though my competence suffers along with the rest of the outsiders — but to suggest that there remains, at least for the time being, a further source of differences between the President and most executive officials: the former cannot fail for long to see what he is up against; the latter have not seen enough of men so placed to have much sympathy or a sure sense for how it feels these days, in these conditions, to be President. What they see with assurance is what they in their jobs want of him in his, a very different matter. Such differing perceptions of the Presidential task are bound to widen differences of perceived need between the White House where responsibility is focused and officialdom where it is not.

The same phenomenon of differing perceptions seems to play a part in other Presidential relationships. No doubt it has some bearing on the current difficulties of relationship between the White House and its counterparts in certain allied capitals where political leaders, in their own capacities, have not experienced the risk to which our President is heir because they lack the power which produced it. Presumably some of the sore spots in Congressional relations have a comparable source. Certainly this is the case with some of the complaints voiced against Messrs. Eisenhower and Kennedy, in turn, by private groups intent upon particular action programs.

The lack of common outlook increases the Presidency's isolation and thus reinforces the dictates of common prudence for a man who bears the burden of that office in our time, namely, to stretch his personal control, his human judgment, as wide and deep as he can make them reach. Your staff report is quite right in its catalog of Presidential needs.

OFFICIALDOM VERSUS THE PRESIDENT

The cold war, however, and the pace of technology have not affected only Presidential needs. They also have affected departmental needs, and in a very different way.

Well before the Soviets achieved ICBM's the pace of change in our own weaponry combined with our wide-ranging economic and political endeavors overseas were mixing up the jurisdictions of all agencies with roles to play, or claim, in national security: mingling operations along programmatic lines, cutting across vertical lines of authority, breaching the neat boxes on organizational charts. Defense, State, CIA, AID, Treasury, together with the President's Executive Office staffs, now form a single complex — a national security complex, if you will — tied together by an intricate network of program and staff interrelationships in Washington and in the field. AEC, ACDA, USIA are also in the complex; others lurk nearby, tied in to a degree, as for example Commerce.

As early as the National Security Act of 1947 we formally acknowledged the close ties of foreign, military, economic policy;

these ties had been rendered very plain by World War II experience. But in the pre-Korean years when ECA was on its own, when CIA was new, when MAAG's were hardly heard of, while atom bombs were ours alone and military budgets stood at under $15 billion, a Secretary of Defense could forbid contacts between Pentagon and State at any level lower than his own, and within limits could enforce his ban. That happened only 14 years ago. In bureaucratic terms it is as remote as the Stone Age.

While operations now have been entangled inextricably, our formal organizations and their statutory powers and the jurisdictions of Congressional committees remain much as ever: distinct, disparate, dispersed. Our personnel systems are equally dispersed. In the national security complex alone, I count at least seven separate professional career systems — military included — along with the general civil service which to most intents and purposes is departmentalized.

These days few staffs in any agency can do their work alone without active support or at least passive acquiescence from staffs outside, in other agencies — often many others. Yet no one agency, no personnel system is the effective boss of any other; no one staff owes effective loyalty to the others. By and large the stakes which move men's loyalties — whether purpose, prestige, power, or promotion — run to one's own program, one's own career system, along agency lines not across them.

These developments place premiums on interstaff negotiation, compromise, agreement in the course of everybody's action. This subcommittee has deplored the horrors of committee work: the wastes of time, the earstrain — and the eyestrain — the "papering over" of differences, the search for lowest common denominators of agreement. I deplore these horrors, too, and freely advocate "committee killing," periodically, to keep them within bounds. But given the realities of programming and operations, interagency negotiation cannot be avoided. To "kill" committees is, at most, to drive them underground. Officials have to find at least an informal equivalent. What else are they to do?

One other thing they can do is push their pet issues up for argument and settlement at higher levels. Once started on this course, there is no very satisfactory place to stop short of the White House. In logic and in law only the Presidency stands somewhat above all agencies, all personnel systems, all staffs. Here one can hope to gain decisions as definitive as our system permits; Congressional committees may be able to supplant them, special pleaders may be able to reverse them, foot-draggers may be able to subvert them — even so, they are the surest thing obtainable.

Accordingly officials urged to show initiative, to quit logrolling in committee, to be vigorous in advocacy, firm in execution, turn toward the White House seeking from it regular, reliable, consistent service as a fixed and constant court of arbitration for the national security complex. This means, of course, a court which knows how courts behave and does not enter cases prematurely. Your staff report rightly describes the sort of service wanted; in the circumstances of officials they do well to want it.

Their need for such a service is unquestionable, and legitimate. To flounder through the mush of "iffy" answers, or evasions; to struggle through the murk of many voices, few directives; to fight without assurance of a referee; to face the Hill without assurance of a buffer; or on the other hand, to clean up after eager amateurs, to repair damage done by ex parte proceedings; to cope with happy thoughts in highest places — these are what officialdom complains of, and with reason. For the work of large-scale enterprises tends to be disrupted by such breaches of "good order" and routine. Not bureaucrats alone but also Presidents have stakes in the effectiveness of the executive bureaucracy. From any point of view, officials surely are entitled to want White House service in support of their performance.

But if a President should give this service to their satisfaction, what becomes of him? While he sits as the judge of issues brought by others — keeping order, following procedure, filing decisions, clearing dockets — what happens to his personal initiative, his search for information, his reach for control, his mastery of detail? What happens to his own concerns outside the sphere of national security? In short, where is his flexibility? The answers I think are plain. Thus the dilemma with which I began: To a degree — a large degree — his needs and theirs are incompatible.

HELP FROM THE SECRETARY OF STATE?

It is tempting to assert that this dilemma could be resolved at a stroke by the appointment of a "czar," a Presidential deputy, to serve as court-of-first-resort for all disputes within the national security complex except the ones the President preempted out of interest to himself or to the Nation. The "solution" is tempting but I find it quite unreal. I do not see how this role can be built into our system. I share the reservations put on record by the reports of your predecessor subcommittee.

Setting aside grandiose solutions, what might be done to ease the tension between Presidential and official needs, to keep the pains of this dilemma within bounds? The answer I believe — insofar as one exists — lies in careful and selective augmentation of the Presidency's staff resources. A President may not need deputies, writ large, to keep decisions from him but he certainly needs ready and responsive staff work in the preparatory phases of decision-making and followup. The better he is served thereby, the better will officialdom be served as well. In this their needs run parallel: effective staff work for him cannot help but put some firm procedure under foot for them; such staff work promises that bases will be touched, standpoints explored — with rocks turned over and the worms revealed — positions traced, appeals arranged, compromises tested. When this prospect is seen ahead official hearts are glad.

In the nature of the case, a President's assistants at the White House cannot do that sort of staff work by themselves except — they hope and so does he — on issues having top priority for him in his own mind and schedule, day-to-day. Preparatory work on issues not yet in that class and followup on issues which have left it must be done, if done at all, at one remove through staff facilities less dominated by the President's immediate requirements. Hence the distinction introduced a quarter-century ago between personal staff at the White House and institutional staff, mainly career staff, in the executive offices across the street, of which the longest-lived example is the Bureau of the Budget.

But in the sphere of national security there is no Budget Bureau. Its nearest counterpart remains the Office of the Secretary of State. This is the traditional source of "institutional" assistance for a President in what was once the peacetime sum of foreign relations: diplomacy. And while the Office has not kept pace with the meaning of that term, no full-scale substitute has been built in its stead. I hope none will be. I hope, rather, that the Secretary's Office can be rebuilt on a scale commensurate with the contemporary reach of foreign relations.

Reliance on the Secretary's Office as an institutional staff resource seems to have been envisaged at the start of Mr. Kennedy's administration. On the White House side Mr. Bundy was named to the necessary personal assistantship, filling a post established in the previous administration: "Special Assistant for National Security Affairs." But formalized committee structures and secretariats built up around his post during the 1950's were scaled down or disestablished by the new administration. This was done with the expressed intent of improving staff performance by transferring staff functions to the Office of the Secretary of State. OCB* is a case in point. As Mr. Bundy wrote your chairman on September 4, 1961:

> It was and is our belief that there is much to be done that the OCB could not do, and that the things it did do can be done as well or better in other ways.
>
> The most important of these other ways is an increased reliance on the leadership of the Department of State . . . the President has made it very clear that he does not want a large separate organization between him and his Secretary of State. Neither does he wish any question to arise as to the clear authority and responsibility of the Secretary of State, not only in his own Department, and not only in such large-scale related areas as foreign aid and information policy, but also as the agent of coordination in all our major policies toward other nations.

For a variety of reasons, some of them beyond my range of observation, this staffing pattern has not been set firmly up to now: the White House side, the "personal" side, seems firm enough but not the other side, the "institutional" side. So far as I can judge, the State Department has not yet found means to take the proffered role and play it vigorously across the board of national security affairs. The difficulties here may be endemic; the role may ask too much of one department among others. But I think it is decidedly too soon to tell. State, I conceive, should have the benefit of every doubt and more time for experiment.

This seems to be the view of the administration. It is striking that in all these months the White House staff has set up no procedures or "machinery" which would interfere in any way with building up the Secretary's Office as a Presidential "agent of coordination." It is striking also that the Secretary has moved toward enhancement of his Office by equipping it with a strong No. 3 position in the person of Mr. Harriman, who preceded me at your hearings. The burdens of advice-giving and of negotiation weigh heavily these days not only on the Secretary but also on the Under Secretary. This position

---

* OCB — Operations Coordinating Board. For a description, see pp. 91–92. — Ed.

thus comes into play as in effect their common deputyship. Mr. Harriman, I take it, with his new authority as second Under Secretary has more opportunity than they to be a source of guidance and of stiffening — and interference-running — for careerists in the State Department, as they deal with one another and with staffs outside. If he actually can do this, if he too is not weighed down by other duties, then the ground may be prepared now for substantial further movement toward development of central staff work in the national security sphere.

Until now, I gather, no one has had time to make himself consistently an energizer, catalyst, connective for the several sorts of planners, secretariats, task forces, and action officers now scattered through the upper floors of our vast new State building. The Secretary may sit at the center of this vastness, but his Office has almost no staff which he can call his own. To weld together such a staff out of these scattered pieces, to imbue it with cohesion and a government-wide outlook, to implant it as a Presidential agent of coordination for the sweep of national security affairs: all this is far from done. I need not tell you why I think the doing will take time.

THE SECRETARY VERSUS THE OTHERS

But I must not mislead you. What I offer here is "conventional wisdom," my hopes are conventional hopes. To call for augmentation of the Presidency's staff resources is to echo what has been prescribed for almost every governmental ailment these past 30 years. To fasten on the Secretary's Office as the means is to follow the footsteps of innumerable study groups intent upon improving something in particular within the range of foreign operations. The Herter Committee very recently, concerned for personnel in Foreign Service, charged the Secretary's Office with coordination of civilian career systems. Now I come along to charge the Office with coordinative staff work in the realm of policy. Such unanimity is dangerous.

The danger is that as we try to make the Secretary's Office serve the needs of personnel directors, or of action officers, or White House aids, or Presidents, we may forget the Secretary's needs. The danger is that as we try to make him a strong instrument for other people's purposes we may forget that he will have some purpose of his own. The modern secretaryship of state is not merely a Presidential staff resource — or a personnel agency for that matter — nor can it be used simply to bridge differences between the President and officialdom. This Office has its own compelling and divergent needs apart from theirs; it has its own dilemma differing from theirs. To seek the best of both worlds from the Secretary's Office, to intend effective staff work for both President and Secretary, is to present as delicate a task of institution building as the Executive has faced in modern times. Because it is so delicate the outcome is uncertain. The danger is that in our advocacy we forget the delicacy, the uncertainty, or both.

Consider for a moment the responsibility of any modern Secretary of State. Always in form, usually in fact, the man becomes a very senior personal adviser to the President, a source of brainpower and judgment for him both as one man to another and at working sessions of his chosen inner circle — currently the executive committee of the National Security Council. Perhaps this was not Mr. Bryan's role — to reach far back — or Mr. Hull's, but certainly it was the role of Messrs. Marshall, Acheson, and Dulles, among others. Under conditions of cold war, this role is sharpened, rendered more intense by emergence of the Secretary of Defense, an officer with roughly equal claim but necessarily different focus, as a source of judgment in the foreign relations sphere. Balance of advice becomes important on each issue every day.

The Secretary of State is much more than a personal adviser. He also is our ranking diplomat at large for sensitive negotiations just short of the summit. Furthermore, he serves as an administration voice to Congress, to the country, and abroad whose public word is weighty in proportion to his rank. At the same time he is actively in charge of a complex administrative entity. He is "Mr. State Department" and "Mr. Foreign Service," leader of officials, spokesman for their causes, guardian of their interests, judge of their disputes, superintendent of their work, master of their careers.

The Secretary of State has a dilemma all his own. These roles are mutually reinforcing: his advice gains weight because he represents the whole Department, his public statements and internal orders gain in potency because he is so often at the White House. But these roles are also mutually antagonistic: Fronting for officials strains his credit as an adviser, advising keeps his mind off management, negotiating preempts energy and time. No modern Secretary has performed the miracle of playing all these roles at once so skillfully and carefully that he obtains the benefits of all and pays no penalties. Presumably there is no way to do it.

A Secretary cannot wriggle out of this dilemma by ditching his department and retreating to the White House, although at least one Secretary may have wished he could. His job cannot be done from there, nor is he needed there. Another man can serve, and does, as White House aide for national security affairs; like others of his kind the aide stays close at hand to deal with action issues on the President's agenda when and how the President's own mind, interests, and work habits require as he meets his own time pressures and priorities. No doubt this personal assistantship includes a role as personal adviser. The Secretary also is a personal adviser. But this coincidence does not make them the same, nor would it help the President to have two such assistants and no Secretary.

The Secretary's usefulness as an adviser lies precisely in the fact that he is more than just another aide whose work is tied entirely to the President's. The Secretary has work of his own, resources of his own, vistas of his own. He is in business under his own name and in his name powers are exercised, decisions taken. Therefore he can press his personal authority, his own opinion, his adviser's role, wherever he sees fit across the whole contemporary reach of foreign relations, never mind the organization charts. He cannot hope to win all arguments in such a sphere, nor is he in position to contest them indiscriminately. But his status and the tasks of his Department give him every right to raise his voice where, when and as he chooses. To abandon his Department in an effort to escape its burdens and distractions is to cloud his title as adviser.

Yet to concentrate on running his department — combating weaknesses, asserting jurisdictions, adjudicating feuds — is no better solution for a Secretary's problem. With the President absorbed, as Presidents must be, in foreign operations, in diplomacy, defense, no Secretary worth his salt would spend much time on management while others drafted cables in the Cabinet room. And if he did he would not long remain effective as a personal adviser.

The modern Secretary of State, whoever he may be, deserves more sympathy than most receive. He lives with his dilemma but he cannot take the comfort which officials, facing theirs, draw from longevity: "This too shall pass." Nor can he take the comfort which a President derives from being, for a fixed term, No. 1. The Secretary's only consolation is to share with Gilbert's Gondoliers "the satisfying feeling that our duty has been done." But "duty" is exceedingly ambiguous for him. What about the duties he has slighted?

Two Notes of Caution

Under these circumstances it would add insult to injury if this man were asked to serve in any simple sense as the Director of a Presidential staff facility on the model of the Bureau of the Budget. For self-protection he would have to shirk the task if it were his. Otherwise he would be kept so busy checking on the work of his resentful Cabinet colleagues that every present role might suffer more than it does now. What is the gain from that? But if we simply move the upper reaches of the State Department out from under him and tie them to the Presidency apart from him, where does he get his staff work done, who bulwarks his initiatives, supports his roles? Yet if we leave his departmental aides to serve him only and turn elsewhere for the Presidency's service — if, as some have urged, we simply set up a new "Office of National Security Affairs" in the Executive Offices beside the Budget Bureau — what happens to the Secretary's status and utility in doing what he now does for our Government?

I pose these questions to be cautious, not equivocal. I hope that through the Secretary's Office we can build an institution serving both the Presidency and the Secretary himself. I hope thereby that we can ease the tension between President and officialdom, and at the same time ease the Secretary's own dilemma. In my opinion we should try to realize these hopes. But I would not pretend to you that such a course is either safe or certain. And assuredly it is not simple.

In closing let me add a second caution: even with time, even with good use of it, even if we master complex institution building, we can expect no miracles from policy. Even if the Secretary's Office should become a partner with the White House in the Presidency's business while the Secretary's business is protected and enhanced, even then both sorts of business would be botched on numerous occasions. For methods and procedures at their best cannot abolish the deep difficulties of perception, of analysis, of judgment, of persuasion which confront our policymakers now and in the future. Organizational arrangements at their most ingenious cannot rub out the underlying differences of duty, interest, role, perspective, separating Presidency from officialdom — and separating both from Congress, for that matter.

These difficulties, differences, lie at the root of most "botched business" we have witnessed in the past and will experience in future. Machinery may confine the damage, or enlarge it, but to see the source of damage as the vehicle in use is to ignore the driver, and his passengers, and road conditions, and the other drivers. To claim that it could be made damageproof by redesign is to divert attention from the human condition. I would make no such claim. Machinery is important; our President and our executive officials need the most effective mechanisms they can get. Still, this remains emphatically a government of men who face in national security affairs unprecedented problems mostly not of their own making.

They dare not hope for too much from machinery, nor should we. To do so is to court unnecessary disappointment. As the world goes these days I see no need for that. There seems to be quite enough necessary disappointment.

4   *The Department of State*

The Department of State is a large and complex organization with internal administrative arrangements that lend themselves to elaborate charts and diagrams. While these diagrams are useful to an understanding of what the Department looks like, they do not tell very much about what the Department does. The following selection, by Charlton Ogburn, Jr., tells us how the personnel in the various boxes in the charts actually behave in relation to a problem and to each other (thus proving that a few thousand words are worth more than one picture).

The Flow of Policymaking in the Department of State

CHARLTON OGBURN, JR.

The Department of State is an organism that is constantly responding to a vast assortment of stimuli. A new Soviet threat to Berlin, a forthcoming conference of Foreign Ministers of the Organization of American States, a request from Poland for credit, a solicitation for support of a candidacy for the Presidency of the United Nations General Assembly, a plea from an ambassador that the head of the government to which he is accredited be invited to visit the United States officially, a refusal by another government to permit the duty-free importation of some official supplies for a U.S. consulate, a request from the White House for comment on the foreign affairs section of a major Presidential address, an earthquake in the Aegean creating hardships which it appears the U.S. Navy might be able to alleviate, a request for a speaker from a foreign policy association in California, a transmittal slip from a Member of Congress asking for information with which to reply to a letter from a constituent protesting discriminatory actions against his business by a foreign government, letters from citizens both supporting and deploring the policy of nonrecognition of Communist China, a continuing inquiry by a press correspondent who has got wind of a top secret telegram from Embassy Bonn on the subject of German rearmament and is determined to find out what is in it, a demand by a Protestant church group that the Department take steps to prevent harassment of their coreligionists in a foreign country, a request by a delegation of a federation of women's clubs for a briefing on southeast Asia and suggestions as to how its members might be use-

Reprinted from Charlton Ogburn, Jr., "The Flow of Policymaking in the Department of State," in *The Formulation and Administration of United States Foreign Policy*, Study No. 9 in United States Foreign Policy, prepared by the Brookings Institution at the request of the Committee on Foreign Relations, United States Senate, 86th Congress, 2nd Session, U.S. Government Printing Office, Washington, D.C., 1960, Appendix C, pp. 172–77.

ful in their planned tour of the area, a request from Consulate General Brazzaville for a revision of cost-of-living allowances, a visit by a commission of inquiry into the operations of U.S. foreign aid programs, a notification from the staff of the National Security Council that a revision of the National Security Council paper on dependent areas is due, a telegram from a U.S. embassy in the Near East declaring that last night's flareups make a visit by the Assistant Secretary for Near Eastern and South Asian Affairs, now in mid-Atlantic, inopportune at the moment, a warning by a European Foreign Minister of the consequences should the United States fail to support his nation's position in the Security Council, and a counterwarning by an African representative at the United Nations of the consequences should the United States do so — this is a sample of the requirements made of the Department of State in a typical day. Of course it does not include the oceans of informational reports that come into the Department by telegram and air pouch or the countless periodicals from all parts of the world that arrive by sea.

What is required to begin with is that the flow be routed into the right channels. This does not apply to press correspondents and foreign embassy officials; they usually know where to go without being directed. For the rest, almost every piece of business — every requirement or opportunity for action — comes within the Department's ken first as a piece of paper. These pieces of paper — telegrams, dispatches (or "despatches," as the Department prefers to call them), letters — must be gotten as speedily as possible into the hands of the officers who will have to do something about them or whose jobs require that they know about them.

The telegram and mail branches of the Division of Communication Services, a part of the Bureau of Administration, receive the incoming material and, after decoding and reproducing the telegrams, indicate on each communication the distribution it should receive among the bureaus or equivalent components of the Department. If, in the case of a letter or a dispatch, there are not enough copies to go around, the recipients are listed one after another and receive it consecutively, the original going first to the bureau responsible for taking whatever action the document requires. With telegrams, the deliveries are simultaneous. Several score copies of a telegram may be run off. A yellow copy, called the action copy, like the original of a dispatch or letter, goes to the bureau responsible for taking any necessary action; white copies go to all others interested.

A telegram (No. 1029, let us say) from a major U.S. embassy in Western Europe reports the warning of the Foreign Minister of X country that a grave strain would be imposed on relations between X and the United States should the latter fail to vote with X on a sensitive colonial issue in the United Nations General Assembly. Such a telegram would have a wide distribution. The action copy would go to the Bureau of European Affairs. The action copy of a telegram to the same purpose from the U.S. delegation to the United Nations in New York, quoting the X delegation, would go to the Bureau of International Organization Affairs. This is a matter of convention.

Information copies of a telegram of such importance would go to all officers in the higher echelons — the Secretary of State (via the executive secretariat), the Under Secretaries, the Deputy Under Secretaries, the Counselor. They would also go to the Policy Planning Staff, to the Bureau of African Affairs because of the involvement of certain territories within its jurisdiction, to the Bureau of Far Eastern Affairs and the Bureau of Near Eastern and South Asian Affairs because the telegram concerns the incendiary question of European peoples' ruling non-European peoples, and of course to the Bureau of Intelligence and Research. Other copies would go to the Department of Defense and the Central Intelligence Agency. The executive secretariat would doubtless make certain that the Secretary would see the telegram. In addition, its staff would include a condensation in the secret daily summary, a slim compendium distributed in the Department on a need-to-know basis. If classified top secret, it would be included in the top secret daily staff summary, or black book, which goes only to Assistant Secretary-level officials and higher.

In the bureaus, incoming material is received by the message centers. There a further and more refined distribution would be made of telegram 1029. Copies would go to the Office of the Assistant Secretary (the so-called front office), to the United Nations adviser, to the public affairs adviser (since the United States is going to be in for trouble with public opinion in either one part of the world or the other), and to whatever geographic office or offices may seem to have the major interest. In the Bureau of International Organization Affairs, this would be the Office of United Nations Political and

Security Affairs. Another copy, however, might go to the Office of Dependent Area Affairs.

In the Bureau of European Affairs, the yellow action copy of the telegram goes to the Office of Western European Affairs and thence to the X country desk, where it is the first thing to greet the desk officer's eye in the morning. As it happens, the desk officer was out the evening before at an official function where he discussed at length with the first secretary of the X embassy the desirability of avoiding any extremes of action in the United Nations over the territory in question. In the front office of the Bureau, the staff assistant has entered in his records the salient details of the problem the Bureau is charged with and has passed the telegram on to the Assistant Secretary.

The following scenes are now enacted:

The X country desk officer crosses the hall to the office of his superior, the officer-in-charge, and the two together repair to the office of the Director of the Office of Western European Affairs. The three officers put in a call to the Assistant Secretary for European Affairs and tell his secretary that they would like as early an appointment as possible.

The Director of the Office of United Nations Political and Security Affairs (UNP) telephones the Director of the Office of Western European Affairs (WE). He says he assumes WE will be drafting an instruction to the U.S. embassy in X to try to dissuade the Foreign Office from its course, and that UNP would like to be in on it. He adds that they had thought of getting the U.S. delegation to the United Nations (US Del) to present this view to the X mission in New York but that there seemed to be no point in doing so since the latter would already be advising its government to take account of world opinion.

After the Secretary's morning staff conference, where the matter is discussed briefly, a conference is held in the Office of the Assistant Secretary for European Affairs to decide on a line to take with the X government. The X desk officer is designated to prepare the first draft of a telegram embodying it. The draft is reviewed and modified by his officer-in-charge and the Office Director for Western European Affairs.

The telegram instructs the U.S. embassy in X to make clear to the X government our fear that its projected course of action "will only play into hands extremists and dishearten and undermine position elements friendly to West" and suggests that the X government emphasize its policy to take account of the legitimate aspirations of the indigenous population of the territory in order to improve the atmosphere for consideration of the problem by the General Assembly. The Assistant Secretary, after scrutinizing and approving the telegram, finds it necessary only to add the Bureau of Near Eastern and South Asian Affairs to the clearances. Those already listed for clearance are the Deputy Under Secretary for Political Affairs, the Bureau of International Organization Affairs, and the Bureau of African Affairs. He says it can be left to the Deputy Under Secretary for Political Affairs to sign the telegram; he does not see that the telegram need go higher.

It remains for the drafting officer to circulate the telegram for approval by those marked for clearance. In the Bureau of African Affairs the telegram is termed extremely gentle to the X government but is initialed as it stands. The Office of the United Nations Political and Security Affairs (UNP) wishes to remind X that the United States, setting an example of its adherence to the principle of affording the widest latitude to the General Assembly, had even accepted on occasion the inscription of an item on the agenda accusing the United States of aggression. The X desk officer states, however, that WE would not favor such an addition, which might only further antagonize the X government. Thereupon, UNP, yielding on this point, requests deletion of a phrase in the telegram seeming to place the United States behind the X contention that the question is not appropriate for discussion in the United Nations. The drafter of the telegram telephones the Director of the Office of Western European Affairs who authorizes the deletion, having decided that he can do so on his own without referring the question to his superior, the Assistant Secretary.

With that, the Director of the Office of United Nations Political and Security Affairs initials the telegram for his Bureau, and the X desk officer "hand carries" the telegram (in the departmental phrase), with telegram 1029 attached, to the Office of the Deputy Under Secretary for Political Affairs and leaves it with his secretary. At 6 o'clock he is informed by telephone that the Deputy Under Secretary has signed the telegram (that is, signed the Secretary's name with his own initials beneath) without comment. The desk officer goes to the fifth floor, retrieves it, and takes it to the correspondence review staff of the executive secretariat, where the telegram is examined for intelligibility, completion of clearances, conformity with departmental practices, etc., before being sped to the Telegram Branch for enciphering and transmission.

The next morning, all offices of the Department participating in the framing of the telegram receive copies of it hectographed on pink outgoing telegram forms. The telegram, bearing the transmission time of 8:16 P.M., has entered history as the Department's No. 736 to the embassy in X. The X desk officer writes "telegram sent," with the date, in the space indicated by a rubber stamp on the yellow copy of the original telegram 1029, and the staff assistant in the front office makes an equivalent notation in his records. The yellow copy is then sent on to the central files, whence in time it will probably be consigned to the National Archives. Only the white copies may be kept in the Bureau's files.

In this case, however, no one is under any illusion that the matter has been disposed of. Scarcely 24 hours later comes a new telegram 1035 from the embassy in X reporting that, while the X government may possibly make some concessions, it will certainly wage an all-out fight against inscription of the item and will expect the United States to exert itself to marshal all the negative votes possible. The question is, what position will the United States in fact take and how much effort will it make to win adherents for its position? No one supposes for a moment that this explosive question can be decided on the bureau level. Only the Secretary can do so — as the Secretary himself unhappily realizes.

At the end of a staff meeting on Berlin, the Secretary turns to the Assistant Secretary for Policy Planning and asks him to give some thought within the next few days to the alternatives open on the question. The official addressed sets the wheels in motion at once. A meeting is called for the next morning. Attending are: the Assistant Secretary for Policy Planning himself and several members of his staff (including the European and African specialists), the Director of the Office of United Nations Political and Security Affairs, the Western European officer-in-charge, the X desk officer, a member of the policy guidance and coordination staff of the Bureau of Public Affairs, and two intelligence specialists, namely, the Director of the Office of Research and Analysis for Western Europe and the Director of the Office of Research and Analysis for the Near East, South Asia, and Africa.

The discussion explores all ramifications of the issues involved and is generally detached and dispassionate. The object of the meeting is to help clarify the issues so that the Policy Planning Staff may be sure all relevant considerations are taken into account in the staff paper it will prepare for the Secretary.

The Secretary is in a difficult position. The President's views on what course of action to take are somewhat different from his. The Congress is also of divided view, with some Members impressed by the irresistible force of nationalism among dependent peoples, others by the essential role of X in NATO and European defense. The ambassadors of some countries pull him one way, others another. One of the Nation's leading newspapers editorially counsels "restraint, understanding and vision." At the staff meeting he calls to arrive at a decision, the Secretary perceives that his subordinates are as deeply divided as he feared. He takes counsel with each — the Assistant Secretaries for Policy Planning, European Affairs, African Affairs, and Near Eastern and South Asian Affairs. At the end he sums up and announces his decision. Thereupon the following things happen:

The Assistant Secretaries take the news back to their bureaus.

An urgent telegram is sent to the U.S. Embassy in X reporting the decision.

Telegrams are sent to embassies in important capitals around the world instructing the ambassador to go to the Foregin Office and present the U.S. case in persuasive terms.

A similar telegram is sent to the U.S. delegation in New York for its use in talks with the delegations of other United Nations members.

Conferences attended by representatives of the geographic bureaus concerned, of the Bureau of Public Affairs, and of the U.S. Information Agency, are held. Afterward, the representatives of the U.S. Information Agency return to their headquarters to draft guidances to the U.S. Information Service establishments all over the world. Such guidances tell how news of the U.S. decision is to be played when it breaks.

The more important the problem, the more the upper levels of the Department become involved. In a crisis — one brought about, say, by the overthrow of A, a Western-oriented government in the Middle East — the Secretary himself will take over. However, the bulk of the Department's business is carried on, of necessity, by the lower ranking officers. Even when a crisis receives the Secretary's personal, day-to-day direction, the desk officer and the officer-in-charge are always at hand to provide the detailed information only specialists possess, while in the intelligence bureau, country analysts and branch chiefs will be putting in 10-hour days and 6- or 7-day weeks. Generally, moreover, the crisis will have been preceded by a good deal of work on the part of lower level officials.

In the case suggested, it was apparent for sometime that all was not well in A. The U.S. Embassy in A was aware of growing discontent with the regime through its indirect contacts with opposition political elements, from information from Cairo, from evidences of tension, from clandestine publications. Additional straws in the wind were supplied by the public affairs officer in A both to the embassy and to the U.S. Information Agency because of his special contacts among professional groups. On the strength of these reports and of dispatches from American foreign correspondents in the area, and equipped with analyses from the Bureau of Intelligence and Research, all pointing in the same direction, the desk officer at a staff meeting of the Office of Near Eastern Affairs imparts his disquiet. He is directed to prepare a memorandum which, if convincing in its presentation, the Office Director undertakes to put before the Assistant Secretary.

What the desk officer has in mind will require national action, so what he drafts takes the form of a memorandum to the Secretary. It embodies a statement of the problem, the actions recommended, a review of the facts bearing upon the problem, and a conclusion. At the end are listed the symbols of the offices of the Department from which concurrences must be sought. Backing up the memorandum will be supporting documents, especially telegrams from the embassy, each identified by a tab. The mass fills a third of an in-box.

The problem is defined as that of strengthening the present pro-Western regime of A. By way of recommendation, the desk officer is especially sensitive to the problems and needs of the country for which he is responsible. He calls for more detachment of the United States from A's rival, B, expediting U.S. arms deliveries to A and the supply of certain recoilless rifles and jet fighter planes the A government has been requesting, support for A's membership in various United Nations agencies, a Presidential invitation to the Prime Minister of A to visit the United States. Much of what the memorandum recommends has to be fought out in the Bureau and even in the Office since it conflicts with the claims of countries (and the desk officers responsible for them) in the same jurisdiction. While neither the Office Director nor the Assistant Secretary doubts that support of B is a handicap in the region, they consider that a proposal for a radical departure would simply doom the memorandum by preventing anyone from taking it seriously.

As it finally leaves the Bureau with the Assistant Secretary's signature, the memorandum is considerably revised, and further change awaits it. The Department of Defense cannot provide the desired recoilless rifles and jet fighters. The Bureau of International Organization Affairs cannot offer any undertakings at this stage with respect to the question of membership in United Nations agencies. The Deputy Under Secretary for Political Affairs rules out a request of the President to invite the A Prime Minister for an official visit because the number of those invited is already too large.

Among recommendations in memorandums to the Secretary, as among salmon battling their way upstream to the spawning grounds, mortality is heavy. Almost everywhere in the world, things are far from satisfactory, but the United States cannot be doing everything everywhere at the same time. And A, far from seeming to cry out for attention, looks like the one Middle Eastern country about which it is not necessary to worry.

Then the uprising occurs in A. Early in the morning, the officer-in-charge of A and one other country is awakened by the ringing of the telephone. In a flash, before his feet have touched the floor, he has visualized every conceivable disaster that could have befallen his area and has picked the overthrow of the monarchy in C as the most likely. Or did the security people find a top secret document under his desk?

On the telephone, the watch officer at the Department tells him that a "Niact" (a night action telegram, which means "Get this one read immediately even if you have to rout someone out of bed") is coming off the machine and it looks serious — he had better come down. En route, the officer-in-charge turns on his car radio and picks up a news broadcast, but nothing is said about A. Uncle Sam has beaten the press agencies.

At the Department, he finds the telegram wholly decoded and reads the hectograph master. There is revolution in A. The top leadership has been either murdered or banished. The officer-in-charge could legitimately awaken the Assistant Secretary, but for the moment it seems there is nothing that can be done, so he decides to hold off until 6 A.M. and then call the Office Director and put it up to him. He does, however, call the A desk officer and tell him to get on his way. To share his vigil beside the watch officer's window there is a representative of the executive secretariat, who will have the telegram ready for the Secretary to read immediately on his arrival. In the Bureau of Intelligence and Research — it being now after 4 o'clock — the morning briefers have arrived to go over the night's take and write up items of importance, with analyses, for the Director's use in briefing the Secretary's morning staff conference. The briefer for the Office of Research and Analysis for the Near East, South Asia and Africa — a GS-11 specialist on India — takes one look at the Niact on A and gets on the telephone to the A analyst.

By the time the Secretary has stepped from his black limousine and headed for the private elevator a good deal has happened. In the Bureau of Near Eastern and South Asian Affairs, everyone concerned with A from the Assistant Secretary down, and including the officer-in-charge of Baghdad Pact and Southeast Asia Treaty Organization affairs and the special assistant who serves as a policy and planning adviser, has been in conference for an hour laying out the tasks requiring immediate attention. Two more Niacts have come in from A, one reporting that so far no Americans are known to have been injured but offering little assurance with respect to the future. The Assistant Secretary has already put in a call to the Director of Intelligence [and] Research to ask that all possible information on the new leader of A and his connections be marshaled and that the Central Intelligence Agency be informed of the need. For the rest, the following represent the Assistant Secretary's conception of what should be done first:

1. The Department of Defense must be apprised of the Department of State's anxiety and be requested to have transport planes in readiness at nearby fields for the evacuation of Americans if necessary in accordance with prearranged plans. There must be consultation on what instruments are available if American lives have to be protected by force.

2. The U.S. embassy in C, a friendly neighbor of A's to which the Niacts have been repeated, will be heard from at any moment, and the Special Assistant for Mutual Security Coordination in the Office of the Under Secretary for Economic Affairs and, also, the Office of International Security Affairs in the Department of Defense will

have to be alerted to the possibility of emergency military assistance for C.

3. Anything in the pipeline for A should be held up. The Special Assistant for Mutual Security Coordination must be advised of this.

4. The possibility of a demonstration by the U.S. 6th Fleet in support of C's independence and integrity will have to be discussed with the Department of Defense.

5. A crash national intelligence estimate will be requested of the Central Intelligence Agency, provided the Agency does not consider the situation too fluid for a formal estimate to be useful.

6. The public affairs adviser will get in touch with the Bureau of Public Affairs, the departmental spokesman and the U.S. Information Agency to agree on the kind of face the United States will put on the affair.

7. The B Ambassador will probably have to be called in and apprised of the critical need for his government's acquiescence in overflights of B for the purpose of getting supplies to C. The B and C desk officers had better get busy immediately on a draft telegram to embassy B (repeat to C) setting forth the case the ambassador should make urgently to the B Foreign Office.

At 9:12, anticipating that he will be called to accompany the Secretary to the White House, the Assistant Secretary instructs his secretary to cancel all his appointments for the day, including one with the dentist but excepting his appointment with the C ambassador. ("Mr. Ambassador, you may assure His Majesty that my Government remains fully determined to support the sovereignty and territorial integrity of his nation.")

At 9:14, 1 minute before the scheduled commencement of the staff meeting, the Assistant Secretary joins his colleagues in the Secretary's anteroom, prepared to hear the estimate of the Director of Intelligence and Research and to give his own appraisal and submit his plan of action.

5   *Personnel for the New Diplomacy*

As the United States has become more deeply involved in world affairs, the Department of State and the Foreign Service have had to meet a growing set of challenges and responsibilities. These new demands have been made more urgent by a rapid increase in the number of countries with which the United States maintains diplomatic relations and in the number of international organizations of which it is a member, and also by an enlarged vision of the kinds of relationships — economic, scientific, social, cultural, as well as political — that are part of the so-called "new diplomacy" of the mid-twentieth century. Since the Second World War a number of efforts have been made to modernize the State Department and the diplomatic service, including the Foreign Service Act of 1946, the Hoover Commission Report of 1949 (Report of the Commission on Organization of the Executive Branch of the Government, February 1949), and the Wriston Committee Report of 1954 (Report of the Secretary's Public Committee on Personnel, May 1954). The most important of the Wriston reforms was a particularly ambitious effort to integrate specialized Civil Service personnel into the Foreign Service at all levels, and to use this enlarged Foreign Service to fill the important professional posts both at home and abroad. In a continuing effort to improve the human talent in the diplomatic field, a Committee on Foreign Affairs Personnel was established in 1961 under private auspices, at the request of Secretary of State Dean Rusk. The Committee, under the chairmanship of former Secretary of State Christian A. Herter, considered the personnel problems and requirements of the State Department, the Agency for International Development (AID), and the United States Information Agency (USIA), and in December 1962 issued its report, Personnel for the New Diplomacy. *Chapter IV of this Report is reprinted here.*

The Kinds and Attributes of Personnel

COMMITTEE ON FOREIGN AFFAIRS PERSONNEL

*"What we need to know is everything there is.
What we need to know cannot be accomplished
in a man's lifetime. But we need to delve deeply
into many fields in order that we as policy makers
can make policy with understanding."* — Dean Rusk
(*in remarks to the Foreign Service Association*).

SUMMARY

In this chapter are presented the Committee's views concerning the attributes and qualifications that are especially to be
sought and cultivated among foreign affairs personnel at professional levels. These are discussed under four categories of need: (a)
general qualities of mind and character, (b) executive ability, (c) specialized functional competences, and (d) area knowledge.

*   *   *   *   *

One striking characteristic of the new diplomacy is the diversity
of activities it encompasses and, therefore, the diversity of skills and
knowledge it requires. It is no longer useful to think of foreign affairs
as a single professional field. Rather, it is a broad spectrum into
which a number of professions, some of the orthodox domestic variety and others peculiar to foreign affairs, must be fitted and modified. Equally striking is the premium this very diversity places on
the capacity to coordinate activities, to synthesize points of view,
and to achieve a sense of unity and common purpose.

The qualitative requirements for successful performance in foreign affairs may be grouped in four basic categories: (a) general
qualities, (b) executive ability, (c) specialized competences, and (d)
area knowledge. These four are not mutually exclusive. Each of the

Reprinted from Chapter IV of *Personnel for the New Diplomacy,* Report of the
Committee on Foreign Affairs Personnel, published by and under the auspices
of the Carnegie Endowment for International Peace on behalf of the Committee
on Foreign Affairs Personnel, Washington, D.C., December 1962.

agencies must develop specialists in the professional fields pertinent to it, and each must develop executives capable of providing leadership. Some of the best executives are drawn from the ranks of the specialists. Moreover, both specialists and executives should possess the general qualities of mind and character essential to effectiveness in foreign affairs, and both must be equipped with deep understanding of foreign environments. Each of the four basic requirements is discussed briefly below.

GENERAL QUALITIES

Discussion of general qualities needed in foreign affairs is clouded by the semantic confusion attending the term "generalist," which has long been associated with Foreign Service Officers. In one sense, "generalist" refers to a man's ability to do a variety of things or to perform satisfactorily any task within the limited universe of tasks for which a particular organization exercises responsibility. Before World War II, this concept could be applied more realistically to the Foreign Service than is true today. Its relevance is now essentially confined to positions in small diplomatic and consular posts.

At times "generalist" is used in referring to an officer engaged in political reporting, analysis, and negotiations. This is, however, misleading, since political officers are often as specialized — and their responsibilities are as specialized — as others in our embassies. In fact, virtually all officers abroad, whether labeled political or not, need a broad understanding of political factors as well as social and economic ones.

In another sense, "generalist" refers to a person with ability to comprehend the ends and means with which an organization is involved and the relation of his own role to the totality of organizational activity. This kind of comprehension is devoutly to be desired in *all* foreign affairs employees, especially those at professional levels.

In a fourth sense, the term is equated with "executive." This practice tends to rob both words of utility. It assumes that the hallmarks of an executive are his ability to perform well a variety of activities and his understanding of the total picture. But useful and necessary as these general qualities may be, they are not the same thing as leadership and managerial ability.

It is important to be clear about the need for seeking out and developing persons who are not only expert in a particular phase or aspect of foreign affairs work, but also possess a breadth of understanding of the objectives and instruments of foreign policy. The professional man in foreign affairs cannot be concerned only with his own field of competence. He must understand and appreciate the role of the other professional fields; he must relate the specific to the general, the part to the whole. Additionally, he should, if he is to assume major responsibilities, develop the happy faculty of grasping essentials and applying his knowledge and skills effectively within and across a range of disciplines. This is the sense in which the Committee considers the term "generalist" useful today.

Any listing of desirable qualities risks committing the "paragon fallacy" of setting up standards that no one person could possibly fulfill. Nevertheless, four qualities appear to the Committee vital in the foreign affairs field. Every effort should be made to seek out, and to develop, persons who possess these qualities:

1. *Zeal for creative accomplishment.* Traditional diplomacy has emphasized observing, reporting, and quiet negotiation. These activities still play an important role in our foreign affairs. At the same time, the new diplomacy relies heavily on operating programs, the techniques of which are still being evolved. The strong program orientations of the United States Information Agency and the Agency for International Development tend to attract persons concerned with the more visible evidences of action; this turn of mind is also becoming more apparent among the Department of State's Foreign Service Officers. The Committee here emphasizes that United States foreign policy today calls for substantial numbers of persons strongly disposed to creative accomplishment and action.

2. *Deep understanding of life and culture at home.* Before he can operate effectively in a foreign environment, the officer overseas must know his own. Recruitment programs should place special emphasis on knowledge of the American heritage and institutions, a knowledge that must be continually refreshed. One of the salutary effects of the Wriston Program is that it facilitated the systematic re-exposure of Foreign Service Officers to the domestic scene. The need for such re-exposure remains a critical problem for AID and USIA. The former agency displays a peculiar imbalance. On the one hand, many of the persons who have been with the foreign assistance program for a substantial number of years run the risk of becoming virtually expatriated. On the other hand, AID uses a great

many short-term specialists who, while they may have deep roots in American society, do not stay overseas long enough to develop any deep familiarity with the foreign society. The danger of cultural expatriation is especially grave in USIA because it is this agency's special responsibility to transmit appreciation of our life and culture.

3. *Ability to communicate effectively across cultural barriers* and to develop a sympathetic understanding of other peoples and their cultural heritages. The art of *cross*-cultural communication requires insight into the foreign environment coupled with retention at all times of one's own national identity. Possession of this quality is made more imperative by the geographic expansion of United States foreign affairs representation abroad, encompassing as it now does most of the less familiar cultures of the world.

4. *Adaptability and flexibility.* The capacity to adjust one's self and one's work to new environments and associations, altered directions in policy, and changing work demands and techniques is particularly crucial in a career foreign service where, of necessity, officers must be prepared to serve at a variety of posts and must expect occasional assignments outside their area of preference or specialization. The importance of this requirement was driven home during the Committee's visits to thirty-two posts abroad. Many of the officers interviewed had experienced rapid shifts in the place and nature of their assignments as well as almost day-to-day shifts in the demands placed upon them in their individual jobs. Clearly, professional foreign affairs work has no place for the rigid or routinized mind or for the person who is unable to adapt to change, however well developed his technical competence may be.

EXECUTIVE ABILITY

The professional fields within foreign affairs are not ends in themselves; they must be subordinated to the demands of policy, and they must be coordinated to the goals of program accomplishment. Leadership in welding specialized capacities to produce decisions and carry out policy objectives calls for a high level of executive talent, above and beyond specialized ability.

The number of positions of command and leadership in foreign affairs at home and abroad is astonishingly high. For example, there are now over one hundred United States diplomatic missions overseas, almost all of which require an ambassador, and most of which include a deputy chief of mission with a comparable scope of responsibility. Some of these are of such size and importance that the key supporting positions in the fields of political, economic, consular, and administrative affairs also qualify as truly executive. There are many consular offices of considerable size and importance outside the capital cities; indeed, some of these are more demanding of executive talents than some of the embassies. AID is conducting programs in approximately eighty countries, and most of these call for a chief and deputy chief of the AID mission; the larger missions require additional administrators with a high order of executive ability. In most countries abroad, the role of the public affairs officers and some deputy public affairs officers in USIA missions requires a high level of executive talent.

The demands are no less striking at home. There are in the State Department approximately two hundred positions in the line of command at the level of deputy office director or higher. Additional officers at comparable levels in AID and USIA would double this figure. All told, about 1,000 positions at the present time in these three agencies, at home and abroad, may properly be considered "executive." This number has been going up rapidly ever since World War II. There is every reason to believe it will continue to rise as new countries emerge, as new international instrumentalities are created, and as new functional fields of concern to the United States develop.

The proportion of top executive positions to the total number of officers who might aspire to those positions is unusually high in foreign affairs. This should be seen as an advantage and an inducement to the officers within the several services and to prospective officers in the future. Few fields of professional activity and few, if any, organizations can offer greater opportunity and greater challenge to their officer personnel than the foreign affairs programs and their agencies.

The requirements for effective leadership in foreign affairs today are unusually demanding and difficult to satisfy. The normal attributes of executive ability in domestic organizations are not the only needs. The executive in foreign affairs must also have: a broad understanding of historical forces and of the interplay of intangibles in the body politic, both at home and abroad; an awareness and sensitivity to the possibilities of, and the means and effects of, social change; and an ability to grasp and utilize the full range of political, economic, military, social, psychological, and scientific instruments in the international field. These requirements cannot be met through experience only in the traditional mold of the diplomat: A striking illustration of the new dimensions of diplomacy is the extent to which economic problems have come to occupy the time of virtually all ambassadors abroad as well as many executives at home. In addition, top executives must comprehend the mechanics of government administration, and be able to use the specialized techniques and procedures of management without letting them become ends in themselves. In using the terms "executive" and "administrative" in this report, the Committee means precisely this combination of an appreciation of higher policy considerations and an ability to use the practical tools of management — the combination required by the new nature of diplomacy.

Many of these qualifications are not readily produced in the normal streams of American experience, and must be developed largely within the organizations themselves. The maintenance of a nucleus of qualified foreign affairs executives demands a career system. But it is clear to the Committee that the traditional career system for Foreign Service Officers in the Department of State is inadequate, and in some respects wrongly directed, to develop some of the qualities needed. The favored route to the top in the Foreign Service has been political work; yet most activity within this field is singularly devoid of supervisory or managerial responsibilities.

In this connection, it is interesting to note that present leadership in the State Department, both at home and overseas, includes only a minority of officers who entered and progressed in the Foreign Service by the orthodox examination route. The table below makes this clear. In the Department in Washington, fewer than one-fifth of the executive positions, deputy office director and above, are now held by examination officers.[1] About 36 per cent are held by officers who entered laterally,[2] and the remainder are filled by Reserve Officers, civil servants, and political appointees. Overseas, some 32 chiefs of mission are examination officers, less than a third of the total and barely more than the 30 who entered laterally. All posts of deputy

[1] The term "examination officers" is used herein to describe those Foreign Service Officers who entered the Service originally by examination at the lowest officer level. They also include three who entered as a result of the Rogers Act of 1924.

[2] These include persons who entered the Service under a variety of midcareer entry programs back to 1939, the largest of which by far was the Wriston Program in the mid-1950's.

chief of mission are filled by Foreign Service Officers, but the majority of these, almost two-thirds, are held by lateral entry officers.

Categories and Modes of Entry of Executives in State Department, 1962

	Department		Field					
Categories and Modes of Entry	Deputy Office Directors and above* (Oct. 1962)		Chiefs of Mission (July 1962)		Deputy Chiefs of Mission (July 1962)		Total	
	No.	%	No.	%	No.	%	No.	%
Foreign Service Officers								
Examination Entry	40	18.8	32	31.7	36	37.5	108	26.4
Lateral: Pre-Wriston	23	10.8	23	22.8	39	40.6	85	20.7
Lateral: Wriston and later	53	24.9	7	6.9	21	21.9	81	19.8
Foreign Service Reserve Officers†	26	12.2	—	—	—	—	26	6.3
Civil Service and Political	71	33.3	39	38.6	—	—	110	26.8
Total	213	100.0	101	100.0	96	100.0	410	100.0

* Includes only positions in the line of command.

† Includes one Foreign Service Staff Officer and three officers on detail from other agencies (two from AID, one from USIA).

Foreign development work is particularly demanding of executive talent. AID programs entail heavy operational responsibilities, and most of them operate exclusively in the areas of the world where the forces of change are moving most rapidly. There is almost no way to obtain experience in the United States in coordinating the special interests of a variety of technical fields and fitting them into the complex, changing needs of total societies. The need for sustained development programs for executives in foreign assistance work is critical.

International information work appears to be a good field in which to develop a broad view, a sensitivity to other cultures, an action frame of mind, and program experience. But, as presently set up, USIA has a more limited opportunity to utilize executive talent than do the other agencies. Moreover, the program of USIA is by nature relatively specialized. Consequently, if its best executives are to qualify themselves for broader leadership posts in foreign affairs, they need at some point to acquire experience outside the Agency itself.

SPECIALIZED COMPETENCES

The variety of professional skills required for the conduct of foreign affairs is in direct proportion to the greatly increased scope, complexity, and magnitude of the United States' role in foreign affairs. Unless the need for specialized competences is fully recognized, especially in initial selection of personnel and in their subsequent assignment, promotion, development, and training, our successes may be more than matched by our failures. It is particularly important that the foreign affairs agencies draw on the best professional resources of the United States and that professional skills not readily obtainable on the outside be nurtured and strengthened by imaginative in-service programs of training and development.

Department of State. The problem of specialization has been acute in the Foreign Service of the State Department for many years. The need for providing efficient and flexible means of acquiring specialists in all fields was recognized in the Foreign Service Act of 1946. Heavy reliance, however, was placed on the Foreign Service Reserve and Foreign Service Staff categories to provide specialists and technicians. The Foreign Service Officer Corps itself was conceived more as a "generalist" arm, the members of which would enter for the most part at the bottom and, if not selected-out, would advance by merit to fill positions of command and leadership.

Every major personnel study of the Foreign Service since the enactment of the Foreign Service Act has called for increased recognition of specialization in the Foreign Service Officer category. The Wriston Committee, in its report of 1954, laid particular emphasis on the need for specialists. Its proposals for enlarging the Foreign Service Officer Corps by the integration of Civil Service, Foreign Service Reserve, and Foreign Service Staff personnel were designed in part to strengthen the specialized capabilities of the career Foreign Service. Other recommendations relating to recruitment, training, career development, and promotion were also aimed at this objective.

In practice, however, the Wriston integration program itself did not materially augment the total personnel resources available to the Secretary of State either in terms of specialists or generalists. Rather, it converted into Foreign Service Officers a large number of employees then in the departmental service and in the Foreign Service Reserve and Staff branches.

As pointed out in Chapter III [of this report], the Department is finding it difficult to attract career-minded specialists to fill some Civil Service positions in Washington. It is also finding it difficult to maintain continuity and develop sustained professional interest among Foreign Service Officers in many of the more specialized phases of the Department's activities. Junior Foreign Service Officers are still largely recruited from the academic disciplines traditionally associated with the Foreign Service — history, international relations, and political science — and there has been a conspicuous short-fall in the fields in which specialization is most needed, such as economics and administration. The proportion of Foreign Service Officer appointments at mid-career levels, a potential source of seasoned specialists, has been declining over the past three years. The promotion system for Foreign Service Officers is commonly regarded as not affording equal prospects for specialists. The substantial increase in the use made of the Foreign Service Reserve is further evidence that the State Department is not meeting its needs for specialized talents through the Foreign Service Officer Corps. In short, the Department does not now have enough qualified people in its career professional Foreign Service in a number of fields, and little replenishment is coming up through the ranks. Fortunately, this condition now appears to be receiving the more thoughtful attention it deserves.

Thus, in retrospect, the Department of State has not yet modified its personnel policies and operations to the extent necessary to achieve the objectives advocated by the Wriston Committee with respect to specialization. While the Department's effectuation of the integration program undoubtedly strengthened the specialized capabilities of the career Foreign Service, at least temporarily, the net effect has been to weaken the depth and continuity of specialized competences in Washington. Furthermore, the nature of the personnel system has encouraged many of those integrated into the Foreign Service Officer Corps to flee from their specializations. There are acute shortages of persons who combine specialized knowledge in the fields listed below with experience and broad understanding of foreign affairs. In all these fields, the needs can be expected to grow in the future:

a. Economists with practical competence in planning economic and social development, including specialists in international trade and other fields.
b. Other social scientists, particularly those equipped to deal with problems of social and political development in the newer nations.
c. Management specialists.
d. Politico-military experts.
e. Persons experienced in international organization affairs.
f. Experts in all aspects of obtaining and analyzing intelligence.

United States Information Agency. USIA does not appear to have significant shortages of persons skilled in the various communications media. There are ample reservoirs of talent to draw on in the United States. The real problem is to find persons skilled in the arts and techniques of persuasion who also know their own society well and are capable of operating effectively in foreign environments. Hence, the needs for "Americanization" and for area and language specialization bear particularly heavily upon USIA.

Moreover, USIA's growing program responsibilities in Asia, Africa, and Latin America are creating needs for new kinds of communications practitioners abroad. In many cases, USIA may have less need for specialists with extensive experience in communications media than for young and energetic persons who can adapt the media to new situations and the unusual conditions prevailing in remote regions. Many of USIA's junior officers appear well suited to this kind of activity. The growing importance of the less-developed regions of the world in USIA's program plans may call for increased informational contributions to modernization programs. Growth in these directions obviously heightens USIA's need for stepped-up emphasis on area specialization and for expanded training programs. It calls for more social-science analysts with knowledge of communications theory and techniques, and for new programs of research into the communications aspects of social and political change.

Agency for International Development. The creation of AID in 1961 was premised upon several concepts that may heavily influence the nature of specialized personnel needs in foreign assistance work. These concepts include: emphasis, in AID's own efforts, on planning and advising other governments, on request, rather than actually operating development projects overseas; maximum encouragement of host-country planning and operating; substantial delegation of authority to regional offices and, through them, to field missions; maintenance of a relatively small permanent core of programmers and specialists; and increasing reliance on the specialized resources of other institutions through means other than direct hire.

How far and how effectively AID will move in these directions remains a matter of conjecture. The numbers and kinds of personnel it will need can be estimated only after the Agency has clarified the policies it will pursue in these regards. There is no question, however, that qualified specialists will be needed in a considerable variety of fields for some time to come. The majority of these will probably be temporary employees, either hired directly by the Agency or obtained through contract arrangements with other employers. There will also unquestionably be a continuing need for a relatively small career core of specialists, qualified in these same functional fields, but capable also of planning, directing, advising, and supervising development activities. In Chapter III [of this report], the Committee has proposed that this nucleus of development specialists be incorporated into the proposed Foreign Development Service. An illustrative list of specialists, divided between those who might properly be regarded as temporary and those who would constitute the career group, is shown [in the table] below.[3]

The concern of this chapter is only for the career group of specialists.[4] It appears essential that this group, comprising the planners, negotiators, advisers, and supervisors of AID programs both at home and abroad, include persons well qualified in their technical fields who are also experienced in, and have an understanding of: the AID program; the objectives and workings of the United States Government; and, particularly, foreign policy and overseas activities.

There is a growing need for recognition of the professional quality of development work and for conscious stimulation of the development aspects of existing professions. Development economics is already established, but such recognition is only beginning in other important development fields such as administration, public health, education, and communications. The establishment of a career serv-

[3] This division is based on a study made in February 1962, in which the distinction between career and temporary was made after an analysis of positions then occupied. The table does not include about 1,700 contract employees utilized on AID projects, over 500 employees of other Federal agencies employed overseas on AID projects, and almost 100 overseas consultants.

[4] Chapter IX deals with non-career specialists for overseas development.

AID Foreign Service Specialists as of February 1962

Personnel Category	Total	Career	Temporary
Agriculture	745	50	695
Industry and Mining	234	34	200
Transportation	96	11	85
Labor	38	9	29
Health and Sanitation	220	16	204
Education	356	52	304
Public Administration	108	43	65
Public Safety	131	26	105
Community Development	47	15	32
Housing	38	16	22
Private Enterprise	13	—	13
Participant Training	87	87	—
Communications Media	86	28	58
Procurement and Supply	65	65	—
Washington Complement	123	—	123°
General and Miscellaneous	90	1	89
Total	2,477	453	2,024

° Includes an unknown number of employees who are "career."

ice as recommended in Chapter III would itself contribute to the professional character of development work. A number of proposals in subsequent chapters of this report should likewise contribute to it.

AREA KNOWLEDGE

The importance of foreign affairs for the United States, and the necessarily strong orientation of our foreign policy in the direction of program accomplishment, requires an understanding of the forces of change in foreign societies of a depth never before contemplated. Area specialization is not itself a profession, except perhaps in the academic world. The foreign environment is the factor peculiar to foreign affairs which requires the modifying and synthesizing of the professions. Area knowledge is a requisite in each professional field of foreign affairs. For those serving overseas, area knowledge frequently needs to be coupled with foreign language competence.

While all three agencies require a high degree of flexibility in the deployment of their personnel, each agency must develop expanded programs of area specialization for virtually all functional fields. This is necessary for the improvement of cross-cultural skills.

The Committee does not have in mind the classic image of the scholar steeped in the culture and history of a region. It is more important that an officer be steeped in the problems of United States foreign policy in a given area and at the same time be able to communicate effectively with people in different strata of foreign societies. He should be better attuned to the changes of today and the past thirty years — particularly in the rapidly evolving regions of Africa, Asia, and Latin America — and he should think in terms of ongoing responsibility for the management of United States interests in the country and region of his specialization.

Area specialization is not new in the Department of State. The European and Latin American "circuits" and the "old China hands" existed well before World War II. More recently, Arabists and Soviet and Eastern European specialists have been developed. The number of Japanese and other Far Eastern and South Asian specialists has grown, and the drive to staff the new African posts is creating specialists in that area. Increasing interest in area specialization stems largely from the feeling of many Foreign Service Officers that a good way to reach the top, in a larger and more diversified service, is to become a "double specialist" — that is, both a specialist in political work and an area specialist.

There is little in the way of articulated policy regarding area specialization, no discernible system for gauging the need for area specialists or for relating area to functional specialization. A consciously designed program stressing continuity, improvement of cross-cultural understanding on the part of all officers, and a sense of individual responsibility for the course of events in various areas and countries is needed.

The same shortcomings are found in USIA and AID, and these agencies are unable to offer even the informal inducements that encourage many Foreign Service Officers to take up area specialization. These agencies may need area specialization even more than the State Department because their programs require them to communicate across cultural barriers to whole populations and to key segments of populations.

Familiarity with an area needs to be supplemented by proficiency in foreign languages. The Department of State (and to a lesser extent USIA) has made significant progress in raising the level and extending the scope of the language competence of its Foreign Service Officers; the Committee believes that the career foreign service personnel of USIA and AID should seek to match the standard of the Department of State.

6 The National Security Council

In the foreign affairs field, the Executive power that the Constitution vests in the President of the United States is in fact delegated to and thus dispersed among several Executive departments and many agencies. The distribution of authority and responsibility in foreign affairs is so widespread that a major effort has to be made to bring this Executive power back together if major international policies are to be made coherently and with the substantial participation and agreement of relevant officials and departments. The method or process by which foreign policy-making is integrated varies from Administration to Administration, depending on the preferences and work habits of Presidents. The National Security Council has been the top-level interdepartmental committee since it was created in 1947. Its importance as the actual device for the coordination and unification of major national security policies, however, has fluctuated greatly. President Eisenhower raised it to its highest levels of responsibility, while President Kennedy treated it routinely, preferring to consult with the relevant department heads individually or in small groups and to use the Presidency itself as the locus of coordination and unification. With an institution whose use is so subject to Presidential whim and rapid change, one can have little assurance that any description of its operating procedures will be up-to-date for very long. I have chosen, consequently, not to try to be up-to-date, but rather to present a richly detailed discussion of how the NSC operated in its period of vigor under President Eisenhower. The problem of interagency policy-making and policy coordination in the foreign affairs field will always be with us, and this essay by Burton M. Sapin illuminates a signal — and a widely criticized [1] — effort to deal with it.

[1] Cf. Subcommittee on National Policy Machinery of the Committee on Government Operations, United States Senate, *Organizing for National Security*, Compilation of hearings, additional studies and materials, and staff reports, 87th Congress, 1st Session, Washington, D.C., U.S. Government Printing Office, 1961, 3 volumes.

The Organization and Procedures of the National Security Council Mechanism

Burton M. Sapin

As background for the main body of this study, the present account sets forth in relatively brief compass the organization and procedures of the National Security Council and the subordinate units attached to it.

A. Statutory Basis

The statutory basis of the Council is the National Security Act of 1947, as amended and as supplemented by various Executive orders and memorandums. The function of the Council, as stated in the act, is: "To advise the President with respect to the integration of domestic, foreign, and military policies relating to the national security so as to enable the military services and the other departments and agencies of the Government to cooperate more effectively in matters involving the national security." There is also a paragraph dealing with the Council's responsibility "to assess and appraise the objectives, commitments and risks of the United States in relation to our actual and potential military power, in the interest of national security, for the purpose of making recommendations to the President in connection therewith. . . ." [1]

The membership provided for in the statute includes: The President, Vice President, Secretary of State, Secretary of Defense, and the Director of the Office of Civil and Defense Mobilization. It is also provided in the act that the following are to attend as advisers

Reprinted from Burton M. Sapin, "The Organization and Procedures of the National Security Council Mechanism," in *The Formulation and Administration of United States Foreign Policy*, Study No. 9 in United States Foreign Policy, prepared by the Brookings Institution at the request of the Committee on Foreign Relations, United States Senate, 86th Congress, 2nd Session, U.S. Government Printing Office, Washington, D.C., 1960, Appendix B, pp. 162–71.

[1] National Security Act of 1947, as amended, Public Law 253, 80th Cong., July 26, 1947 (61 Stat. 495), secs. 101 (a) and (b).

to the Council: The Chairman of the Joint Chiefs of Staff and the Director of the Central Intelligence Agency. The Central Intelligence Agency is made directly responsible to the Council.

Before proceeding to a more detailed description of the Council machinery, it should be emphasized that, in the 12 years of its existence, the Council has undergone considerable change and adjustment in its purposes and functions, in its organizational structure, and in its procedures. Furthermore, growth and development still continue. Primary attention in this paper will be given to the present pattern although major trends will be noted.

B. PRESENT ORGANIZATION BRIEFLY DESCRIBED

The National Security Council is a part of the Presidential staff organization known as the Executive Office of the President. The Council has always had a small professional staff attached to it, headed by an executive secretary, performing the following functions — analyzing policy questions independently and in cooperation with relevant agencies, arranging the agenda for meetings, providing and distributing the supporting papers including records of the actions taken at Council meetings, and facilitating negotiations among the participants. While the essential function of the staff is to service the Council, it also provides for the President's Special Assistant for National Security Affairs an "objective analysis of every policy paper that goes through the Planning Board to the Council." While it "does not itself make policy recommendations, it does scrutinize departmental proposals and suggest policy alternatives or additions that merit consideration." [2]

[2] Gordon Gray, Special Assistant to the President for National Security Affairs, "Role of the National Security Council in the Formulation of National Policy," p. 13, unpublished paper presented at the September 1959 meeting of the American Political Science Association in Washington, D.C.

Other useful items on this topic are: Donald S. Bussey, "The National Security Council," December 15, 1958, an unpublished staff paper prepared for the President's Committee to Study the U.S. Military Assistance Program (the "Draper Committee"); Colonel Bussey's paper has an excellent bibliography on the subject; two articles by a former Special Assistant, Robert Cutler, "The Development of the National Security Council," Foreign Affairs, Vol. 34, April 1956, pp. 441–458, and "Defense Organization at the Policy Level," General Electric Defense Quarterly, Vol. 2, January–March 1959, pp. 8–15; William R. Kintner, "Organizing for Conflict: A Proposal," Orbis, Vol. 2, Summer 1958, pp. 155–174; Paul H. Nitze, "National Policymaking Techniques," SAIS Review, Vol. 3, Spring 1959, pp. 3–8; and relevant chapters in Edward H. Hobbs, Behind the President (Washington, 1954), and Timothy W. Stanley, American Defense and National Security (Washington, 1956).

Mr. Cutler refers to the staff as having 11 "think people" who are "scrupulously nonpolitical and nonpolicymaking. They form the backbone of continuity, the reservoir of past knowledge and the staff assistance required by the special assistant in discharging his responsibilities to the President." [3]

According to Colonel Bussey, the total permanent staff in March 1953 numbered 23, including 6 "think people." At Mr. Cutler's recommendation, 5 additional "think people" were added at that time and a total staff of 28 has continued to the present time. [4]

Since 1950 the Council has had a second-level group connected with it which has done much of the work involved in preparing for its consideration policy papers which, if favorably received by the Council and approved by the President, become official policy. This group was known as the Senior Staff under President Truman and became the Planning Board under President Eisenhower. Each member of the National Security Council is represented on the Planning Board, usually by an official of Assistant Secretary rank. In recent years, these officials have relied on a group of their subordinates, the Planning Board assistants, to do much of the detailed drafting.

In late 1953, in part as an outgrowth of a concern to maximize the psychological impact of U.S. policy, still another unit, the Operations Coordinating Board, was made a part of the national security organization, but it was not formally added to the National Security Council structure until July 1957.* In brief, its function is to advise with the agencies concerned to ensure that the interagency execution of policies and programs in various functional and geographical areas is integrated to achieve maximum advantage. The Board is chaired by the Under Secretary of State; other designated members are the Deputy Secretary of Defense, the Director of the Central Intelligence Agency, and the Director of the U.S. Information Agency and the International Cooperation Administration. The Joint Chiefs of Staff are not directly represented.

The Operations Coordinating Board has its own professional staff, headed by an Executive Officer and somewhat separate from

---

[3] Cutler, *Foreign Affairs, op. cit.*, p. 455.

[4] Bussey, *op. cit.*, p. 45.

* The Operations Coordinating Board was subsequently abolished by President Kennedy; see Richard Neustadt's statement, p. 57 *supra*, for the reasons. — Ed.

the staff of the National Security Council-Planning Board structure. Since 1957, there has also been a Presidential Special Assistant for Security Operations Coordination, who is designated Vice Chairman of the Board. This official also attends the meetings of the National Security Council and serves as an adviser to the Planning Board. The Coordinating Board members also have their Board assistants to do preliminary labors for them. Detailed scrutiny of policy execution in various geographical and functional areas is actually carried out by approximately 50 Operations Coordinating Board working groups, interdepartmental committees of working-level officials with 1 professional staff person from the Board's staff also sitting in as a member.

One of President Eisenhower's important innovations in the National Security Council system was to establish in 1953 as part of his own immediate staff the position of Special Assistant to the President for National Security Affairs. This official plays a key role in the meetings of the Council, sits as Chairman of the Planning Board (a role previously played by the Executive Secretary of the Council staff), and is a member of the Operations Coordinating Board.

C. MEMBERSHIP AND MEETING PROCEDURE OF THE COUNCIL

In addition to the statutory members, the Secretary of the Treasury, under both President Truman and President Eisenhower, has had virtually regular membership status. At present, the Director of the Bureau of the Budget and the Chairman of the Atomic Energy Commission also attend the Council meetings on a regular basis. A considerable number of other officials normally are present. Some are staff aides and sit in the outer circle. Mr. Gordon Gray, the present Special Assistant for National Security Affairs, recently provided the following list of these other officials:

"The Assistant to the President; the Director, U.S. Information Agency; the Under Secretary of State; the Special Assistants to the President for Foreign Economic Policy and Science and Technology; the White House Staff Secretary; the Special Assistant to the President for Security Operations Coordination; the Executive Secretary and the Deputy Executive Secretary, National Security Council. For agenda items which are the subject of official interest to them, the Attorney General and the Administrator, National Aeronautics and Space Administration, are invited. Of course, for any agenda

items that the President may determine, ad hoc members participate." [5]

For example, when matters relating to the Military Establishment
are under discussion, the Chiefs of Staff and civilian Secretaries of
the three services are . . . likely to be present. The total of those
now regularly in attendance at Council meetings is 20.

"The Council regularly meets each Thursday at 9 A.M. Meetings
normally do not exceed 2 hours. Special Council meetings are called
by the Special Assistant for National Security Affairs at the request
of the President. The agenda for a Council meeting is determined
by the President, acting through the Special Assistant for National
Security Affairs.

"One feature of every Council meeting is a regular briefing by the
Director of Central Intelligence. He gives a summary of important
developments that are occurring throughout the world, and he gives
particular attention to those areas which are on the Council agenda
that day." [6]

Under President Truman, the Council, particularly in its early
years, did not meet quite so regularly or frequently, although during
the Korean war it began to meet on a regular weekly basis. As Mr.
Cutler has pointed out, President Truman attended the meetings
less regularly than President Eisenhower, who has rarely missed a
meeting since he has been in office, aside from his periods of illness.

The Council may have one item on its agenda or as many as four
or five. There are no formal votes; the usual procedure is to take
"the sense of the meeting." The nature of the Council's procedures
in dealing with the papers that come before it is discussed below.

D. Relationship of the Council to Other Units

Since there are other advisory councils and committees at the
Presidential level and other units in the Executive Office of the President, the question of the Council's relations with them and the division of labor on national security problems is an important one.

The Cabinet is supposed to concern itself with all domestic matters
not bearing "directly and primarily" on national security. This is not
always an obvious or simple distinction, and there are certainly pos-

[5] Gray, *op. cit.*, p. 5.
[6] *Ibid.*, p. 6.

sibilities for jurisdictional dispute. Mr. Robert Cutler indicates how the question has been dealt with under the Eisenhower Administration:

"The complexity of modern times often makes it difficult to draw a clear line between the two categories; but in practice a rational accommodation has invariably been worked out between the Secretary of the Cabinet and the Special Assistant for National Security Affairs." [7]

In other words, the fact that the President now has on his immediate staff both a Special Assistant for the Council and a secretary to the Cabinet provides the opportunity for close cooperation and apparently, under present circumstances, satisfactory working relations.

The question of division of labor also arises regarding those national security matters that might be termed current operational questions and those with important longer term policy aspects and implications, the latter presumably being the special province of the National Security Council. Here again, the present system seems to operate satisfactorily because of good working relationships between the Special Assistant for National Security Affairs and officials like the President's Staff Secretary, who is largely responsible for White House liaison with the Military Establishment on current operational matters.

As to other high-level advisory councils and committees in the foreign policy-national security field, no significant difficulties of integration and coordination seem to have arisen. The National Aeronautics and Space Council, formally chaired by the President, has not been in existence long enough for any important patterns to develop. Both the National Advisory Council on International Monetary and Financial Problems and the Council on Foreign Economic Policy seem to have fairly well-defined areas of responsibility which either have not interfered with any important National Security Council responsibilities or have been brought into the Security Council when this seemed desirable.

In any event, according to the accounts of Mr. Gray and Mr. Cutler, the present President is inclined to give major national security policymaking responsibilities to the Council machinery and to regard exceptions to that rule as temporary.

[7] Cutler, *General Electric Defense Quarterly, op. cit.*, p. 9.

E. Organization and Functions of Other National Security Council Units

It has already been pointed out that one of President Eisenhower's major innovations in the machinery of the Council was the introduction of the position of Special Assistant to the President for National Security Affairs. This official now plays a central role in the operation of the whole structure, excepting only the work of the Operations Coordinating Board. Mr. Gray himself has provided what is probably the most complete and yet succinct summary of the present duties and responsibilities of the Special Assistant:

"Responsibility for agenda, and presentation of material for discussion at Council meetings; as necessary, briefing the President before Council meetings on agenda items; determining, in collaboration with the NSC Executive Secretary, the agenda and scheduling of work for Planning Board meetings; presiding at, and participating in, Planning Board meetings; supervising the work of the NSC staff through the Executive Secretary; attending and participating in meetings of the Operations Coordinating Board, the Council on Foreign Economic Policy and other relevant groups; attending as an observer at meetings of the Cabinet; and such other assignments related to national security affairs as the President may direct." [8]

The general role and organization of the Planning Board have already been noted. Its membership is composed of representatives and observers from the departments and agencies represented on the Council, whether statutory or not. For example, at present a special assistant to the Secretary of the Treasury and an Assistant Director of the Bureau of the Budget sit on the Board. Also present is an officer representing the Joint Chiefs of Staff. It is clear that under present arrangements the Special Assistant for National Security Affairs plays a key role in the work of the group. Under both Mr. Truman and Mr. Eisenhower, there seems to have been the hope that the Senior Staff-Planning Board could be developed into a working team of high-level departmental officials who would devote a substantial portion of their time and efforts to its activities. In both cases, this hope has been disappointed. For those who represent their agencies on the Planning Board, this is but one among a number of very important and time-consuming responsibilities and, usually, just one among a number of very important meetings that

8 Gray, *op. cit.*, p. 8.

must be regularly attended each week. Indeed, a standard complaint is that not infrequently these officials must miss Board meetings and are themselves represented by subordinates. Under Mr. Eisenhower, it has even been necessary to organize a body subsidiary to the Board to do some of its work for it — the Planning Board assistants. The meetings of the Board assistants are not regularly scheduled, but they average about five sessions a month.

Under Mr. Cutler, the Planning Board was meeting regularly on a three-times-a-week basis. Mr. Gray informs us that the Board now meets regularly twice a week, on Tuesday and Friday afternoons "from 2 o'clock till 5 — or such further time as I may keep them in session." [9] Apparently the latter comment is not a mere idle remark because Planning Board sessions have a reputation among those who attend them of lasting often far longer than the scheduled 3 hours.

The Operations Coordinating Board follows a somewhat different pattern. It convenes "at an informal luncheon meeting each Wednesday in the Department of State. The luncheon is attended by the designated members and the Executive Officer [i.e., of the Board staff]; other officials are invited as required for discussion of specific subjects. Thereafter the Board convenes in formal session for the transaction of business indicated in the advance agenda.

". . . A typical meeting includes the following principal items:

"(a) Reports indicating general effectiveness of assigned national security policies and future problems and difficulties in its implementation, for transmittal to the NSC.

"(b) Operations plans for specific countries or regions, as developed by OCB working groups or committees to facilitate effective interdepartmental coordination.

"(c) Special reports for either the Board or the Council by OCB working groups or committees, on their own initiative or by request, analyzing a specific problem and proposing action.

"(d) Oral reports to clarify issues or stimulate discussion." [10]

In addition to the two Presidential special assistants and the other designated members noted earlier, the Under Secretary of the Treasury and the Chairman of the Atomic Energy Commission regularly

[9] Gray, *op. cit.*, p. 7.

[10] Operations Coordinating Board, *Functions and Organization of the Operations Coordinating Board*, February 1958, points 6, 8, 9, and 10. This is a descriptive handbook prepared by the Executive Officer of the Board.

attend the weekly meetings. The Board assistants, who do the "final staff work on subjects to be considered by the Board," meet regularly every Friday. The 50-odd working groups of the Board meet as frequently as is required by their work. They may meet as little as once a month; on the other hand, when they are in process of developing or reviewing an operations plan, they may be meeting on an almost daily basis and devoting a great deal of their time to the work of the interdepartmental working group.

F. The Use of Outside Consultants by the Council

There has been much discussion regarding the desirability of using nongovernmental consultants and advisers in the work of the National Security Council and even some vagueness regarding the actual patterns in this matter. Mr. Gray reports that "from time to time the President appoints one or more consultants as informal advisers to the Council . . . as a general rule, such consultants appear at a Council meeting only to present and discuss their report." He goes on to say:

Examples of the use of such consultants are:

(1) to consider and report to the Council on some proposal, either specific or general, after which the consultant's report is reviewed by the departments and agencies concerned.

(2) to review for the Council integrated recommendations proposed by the NSC Planning Board.

"In the course of the review of a recent fundamental policy paper, 23 consultants were used. They first met with the Planning Board in groups of four or five at a time and gave their views on the existing paper up for review. Then the Planning Board devoted all or part of 27 meetings over many weeks to producing a revised paper, taking into account the comments of the consultants and the recommendations of the responsible agencies. Subsequently, a large number of the consultants came in again, met in a body with the Planning Board, and made further comments on the Planning Board's revised draft. In this way several of the ideas of the consultants formed the basis for policy guidance which was ultimately incorporated into the final approved paper."

Mr. Gray also notes that the reconstitution of the President's Science Advisory Committee and its elevation in December 1957 to a position directly advisory to the President (and, presumably, the simultaneous appointment of a scientific adviser to the President) has diminished the need for outside consultants to the Council and for certain kinds of formalized reports from them.[11]

In his published writing, Mr. Robert Cutler has pointed out a number of the difficulties involved in the use of nongovernmental advisers in the work of the Council. Nevertheless, he reports that during the 3¾ years he was Special Assistant for National Security Affairs, "we drew from resources outside of Government, in many instances from private industry, as many as 15 different consultant groups to assist the NSC mechanism in formulating and reviewing policies. Some of these groups worked over long periods of time and their services became known to the public, such as the Technological Capabilities Panel headed by Dr. Killian in 1954–55, and the Security Resources Panel, the 'Gaither Committee,' in 1957–58. And there were other groups, happily not so well publicized, who gave the benefit of their time and judgment in a stimulating and most helpful way."[12]

G. RELATED DEPARTMENTAL ARRANGEMENTS

Each agency participating in the National Security Council structure has developed some specialized staff arrangements and designated personnel to deal with the flow of documents and substantive problems emerging from its activities. The Vice President also has on his staff an aide responsible for National Security Council matters.

1. *Department of State.* Within the Department of State, the Policy Planning Staff is the unit designated to handle National Security Council and Planning Board matters. The Assistant Secretary who is director of the staff is also the Department's representative on the Planning Board. Within the staff, there are two officers who work full time on Council and Planning Board matters; one acts as alternate to the Assistant Secretary for the Planning Board and the other represents the Department on the Planning Board assistants group. Much of the actual drafting of policy papers for the Planning Board is done in the appropriate geographical or functional units of the Department, working closely with members of the Policy Planning Staff. Since members of the Council staff have reasonably good working relations with these units, as well as with the Department's intelligence bureau, the procedures involved

[11] Gray, *op. cit.*, pp. 5–6.
[12] Cutler, *General Electric Defense Quarterly, op. cit.*, p. 15.

in developing a draft document are presumably well developed and well established and should raise no special difficulties.

The Under Secretary of State has on his immediate staff an officer designated as special assistant for Operations Coordinating Board matters. He is the Department's representative on the Operations Coordinating Board assistants group and works with the Department's representatives on the various Board working groups, which are in fact usually chaired by the Department of State's representative.

2. *Department of Defense.* Although the Deputy Secretary of Defense is the formally designated representative of the Department of Defense on the Operations Coordinating Board, there was a recent period when the Assistant Secretary for International Security Affairs in actual fact represented the Department of Defense on both the Planning Board and the Operations Coordinating Board. He still acts as the Deputy Secretary's alternate on the Coordinating Board, and at times attends meetings of the Security Council itself with the Secretary of Defense. One of his three Deputy Assistant Secretaries is specifically designated as responsible for National Security Council affairs.

The participation of the Chairman of the Joint Chiefs of Staff in the Council is supported by a small staff within the Joint Staff, usually headed by a general or flag officer of two-star rank. This officer is the Joint Chiefs of Staff representative on the Planning Board. He also attends all the meetings of the Joint Chiefs so that he is presumably in a position to reflect their thinking in Planning Board discussions. The Joint Chiefs have no representation per se on the Operations Coordinating Board.

Under the Deputy Assistant Secretary charged with National Security Council affairs, there are specific offices, with quite small combined civilian-military staffs of several persons, dealing with National Security Council affairs and Operations Coordinating Board affairs. The Deputy Assistant Secretary is the Assistant Secretary's alternate for Planning Board meetings. The Director of the Office of National Security Council Affairs is the Department of Defense representative at the Planning Board assistants meetings, while the Director of the Coordinating Board office sits as Defense Department member of that Board assistants group.

The three services themselves have specifically designated units or officers responsible for National Security Council and Operations

Coordinating Board matters. In the Army staff, under the Deputy Chief of Staff for Operations, and, more specifically, the Director for Plans, there is a Special Assistant for National Security Council Affairs — at present a full colonel — who is at the same time chief of the International and Policy Planning Division of the staff. Operations Coordinating Board matters are handled separately by a Special Assistant for Operations Coordinating Board Affairs in the Office of the Director for Operations. The International and Policy Planning Division is in effect the international security affairs staff for the Army Chief of Staff and has approximately 20 action officers, any of whom may work on Planning Board drafts depending upon the subject matter.

The Air Force has an International Affairs Division set up very much like the Army's under the Director of Plans, Deputy Chief of Staff, Plans and Programs. However, at present, the Air Force does have an officer specifically designated as Assistant for National Security Affairs who plays a coordinating role. Most of the work on drafts is done by action officers within the International Affairs Division.

The Navy is organized and operates somewhat differently in this field. All National Security Council and Operations Coordinating Board matters are handled by the Politico-Military Policy Division (Op–61), headed by a rear admiral, under the Deputy Chief of Naval Operations, Plans and Policy. Within this unit, there are different officers responsible for the Planning Board and the Operations Coordinating Board. Since the Navy does not use the action officer technique in this field, drafts are circulated to the relevant units within the over-all Navy staff for comments, which are then pulled together by the responsible officers within Op–61.

3. *Other Agencies.* While the Departments of State and Defense are the most important participating agencies in the structure and have the most substantial arrangements for supporting this participation, the general pattern is similar in other agencies. For example, the Under Secretary of the Treasury represents the Treasury Department on the Operations Coordinating Board and a special assistant to the Secretary of the Treasury sits on the Planning Board. Similar arrangements are found within the Bureau of the Budget.

H. DEVELOPMENT OF A NATIONAL SECURITY COUNCIL PAPER

The usual end product of the work and deliberations of the Planning Board and the Council is a National Security Council policy paper dealing with the particular problem, geographical area, or functional question. Each paper, when finally approved by the President, has some specific numerical designation and is classified as top secret with only a relative handful of numbered copies in circulation. The routine format of these papers was described several years ago by Mr. Robert Cutler in the following terms: "the covering letter, the general considerations, the objectives, the courses of action to carry out the objectives, the financial appendixes, the supporting staff study; for they invariably appeared in this sequence in the final document."[13] It is often the case that a national intelligence estimate on the particular situation or problem will be requested from the Central Intelligence Agency and thus become a part of the documentation.

Gordon Gray distinguishes three types of National Security Council papers: "fundamental policy; geographical policy, on a single foreign country or on a region; and functional papers not related to a specific geographical area."[14] As an example of the continuing experimentation and the developing character of the Council structure, a rather recent innovation has been the "special discussion paper" which Mr. Gray describes in the following terms:

"Additionally, on many occasions the Planning Board will present to the Council, without recommendations, a special discussion paper consisting of a series of seemingly feasible alternatives, with the pros and cons of each carefully set forth. The Council will discuss the alternatives and thereby provide guidance to the Planning Board as a basis for developing a draft policy statement."[15]

The original impetus which leads to a new policy paper or the review and revision of a paper already in existence may come from a number of sources. The President himself, or some other member of the Council, may ask the Planning Board to look into a question and come up with a draft paper if this proves desirable. In the course of its periodic assessments of U.S. policies and programs, the Operations Coordinating Board may conclude that a review of existing policy in some particular area is in order and may so recommend to the Council. The President's Special Assistant for National Security Affairs may himself initiate consideration of some matter. The development may start within one of the participating departments,

---

13 Cutler, *Foreign Affairs, op. cit.,* p. 446.
14 Gray, *op. cit.,* p. 7.
15 *Ibid.,* p. 11.

perhaps even rather far down in the organizational hierarchy. Most obviously, the process may be triggered by some compelling event on the international scene.

However the process is initiated, the request or suggestion is usually turned over to the Planning Board which in turn will ask one of the participating departments to prepare a first draft. Since most of the papers fall into the broad category of foreign policy, the Department of State normally prepares the original draft document. The Council does consider major military policy questions and in those cases, of course, the first draft is likely to be produced by the Military Establishment.

Within the State Department, as indicated above, the draft paper will probably be a joint product of members of the interested bureaus and offices and of the Policy Planning Staff. At times, there may be informal consultation even at this stage with opposite numbers in other departments, such as Defense and Treasury. When the draft has been completed, it will be circulated to the representatives of the other agencies, and then the matter will be placed on the agenda of the Planning Board, presumably allowing enough time for the other participating agencies to develop their views on the paper. However, a frequent complaint is that often there is not enough time available between receipt of the drafts and discussion in the Planning Board to prepare adequate papers on the particular problems.

Since the Military Establishment probably has the most elaborate machinery for developing views on Planning Board papers, it may be useful to trace the progress of one of these papers through the Pentagon. They travel through two separate channels, the Joint Chiefs of Staff organization and the Office of International Security Affairs in the Department of Defense. The responsible Deputy Assistant Secretary of Defense for International Security Affairs and the official under him who deals specifically with National Security Council and Planning Board matters meet weekly with the representatives of the three service staffs referred to earlier to brief them on upcoming Planning Board agenda items and the latest Board actions. These service representatives receive from the International Security Affairs officials the draft Planning Board documents, on which they are asked to comment. After they have developed their positions, their comments are sent to both the Deputy Assistant Secretary and to the two-star officer who is the Joint Chiefs of Staff representative on the Planning Board. While these two officials do consult on Planning Board matters and generally arrive at a common position, it does occasionally happen that there will be disagreement between them at the Planning Board level, the Council level, or both.

The draft policy paper will then be the subject of considerable discussion in the Planning Board. The Special Assistant, acting as chairman and with no departmental viewpoint to defend, is in a position to sharpen the discussion, clarifying areas of agreement and disagreement. The paper may be sent back to the originating department for redrafting, or other departments may contribute drafts of their own. After some discussion in the Board, it may be turned over to the Board assistants for further study and redrafting. Mr. Gray comments: "After the Planning Board has discussed a paper, it is usually turned over to the Board assistants to be redrafted. Normally the Board assistants meet 4 to 8 hours on a paper before sending a redraft back to the Planning Board." Gray describes the procedures of the Planning Board in the following terms:

"Normally, consideration of a geographical policy starts off with a study of the latest national intelligence estimate on the country and a briefing by the CIA adviser on the most recent developments in the area. The Planning Board normally does not send a paper forward without meeting three or four times on it. However, in crisis situations the Planning Board may have to complete a paper in one meeting; and on occasion the NSC has had to take action without referring the matter to the Planning Board at all.[16]

". . . [N]o departmental representative is reticent in marshaling the arguments in support of any position he sees fit to take. Moreover, it is the established practice for Planning Board members to bring experts from their own staffs. For example, when a paper on a foreign country is being discussed, the State Department will bring the area people concerned and the Defense Department may bring the people who deal with the military assistance programs."[17]

Mr. Cutler comments: "The number of times a particular subject comes before a Planning Board meeting depends upon its importance and complexity. A dozen meetings or more may be necessary before the final version of a particular statement is acceptable to the Board."[18]

The draft policy paper prepared by the Planning Board is usually

[16] *Ibid.*, p. 7.
[17] *Ibid.*, p. 9.
[18] Cutler, *General Electric Defense Quarterly, op. cit.*, p. 10.

circulated to the members of the Council 10 days in advance of the time it will be discussed at the Council meeting. Among other things, this 10-day period gives the Joint Chiefs of Staff time to meet and discuss the paper and prepare written comments on it, which are then also circulated in advance to Council members. Usually, members of the Council are briefed on the various agenda items by their own agency representatives on the Planning Board sometime before the meeting.

Under present circumstances, according to Mr. Gray, the "President looks to the Special Assistant at Council meetings to present the items upon the agenda, to brief the Council on their background, to explain any 'splits' and to initiate discussion."[19] With regard to "split papers," Mr. Gray states:

"It is true that despite the best efforts of the Chairman of the Planning Board, policy papers go to the Council from time to time with split recommendations on minor issues. It is not true that major splits are not generally reflected in such papers. In fact, more than half the policy statements which are sent to the Council from the Planning Board contain split views largely on important issues on which one or more of the NSC agencies have indicated a strong divergence of opinion. A recent paper dealing with a fundamental policy contained 19 splits when it was sent to the Council from the Planning Board and required 5 successive Council meetings before final approval."[20]

According to Messrs. Dillon Anderson, Cutler, and Gray — the three men who have served as Special Assistants for National Security Affairs under President Eisenhower — there is often vigorous discussion and exchange of views at the Council table, very much encouraged by the Chairman, the President. Some observers feel that the past two Secretaries of State, Dean Acheson and John Foster Dulles, combining great personal ability and intellectual force with extremely close relations with their Chief Executives, tended to dominate Council discussions.

Mr. Gray also reports: "It is seldom that arguments are made in the Council — except by the President or Vice President — which have not been previously discussed in the Planning Board; although I will say that Council members do not always fully espouse the position taken by their Planning Board representatives and are

[19] Gray, op. cit., p. 8.
[20] Ibid., p. 11.

sometimes persuaded by their own wisdom or by the persuasiveness of others to a different view."[21]

While items may occasionally stay on the Council agenda for several meetings, a decision is usually reached on a particular paper at the same meeting at which it has been presented and discussed. Presumably, after hearing the views of his departmental chiefs and top advisers, the President will reach his own decision, and in the process resolve such differences or splits as may have been present in the original paper. It seems reasonable to assume that the split papers are likely to be among those demanding more than one meeting and discussion. However, Mr. Cutler reports:

"The statement of our basic national security policy, to which all our other security policies are subsidiary, is reviewed annually in the Council. Frequently this searching review will extend, as it did in the 1958 calendar year, over a period of several months. It may require a dozen Planning Board meetings and appear on the agenda of several meetings of the National Security Council."[22]

No formal votes are taken at the Council meetings. After each meeting, a written record of action is prepared for each Presidential decision made and is then circulated in draft to "those who were present at the meeting for comment before" it is submitted "to the President for his consideration, change if necessary, and final approval."[23]

If the approved policy paper involves foreign operations, the usual procedure is for it to be turned over to the Operations Coordinating Board. The Board has no command authority; its work rests on the voluntary cooperation of the participating agencies. If the approved policy deals with a functional or geographical area not previously dealt with in the Operations Coordinating Board machinery, a new interdepartmental working group may be established to coordinate policy and program implementation. Otherwise, an established working group will be given responsibility for the paper. In either case, the working group will probably prepare an operations plan. "In general, this is a comprehensive and fairly detailed outline of operating guidance for implementing a given policy and a listing of what is being done or programed to translate the policy into effective action. When conditions obtaining at the

21 *Ibid.*, p .9.
22 Cutler, *General Electric Defense Quarterly, op. cit.*, p. 11.
23 *Ibid.*

moment are confused or rapidly changing, however, only the operational guidance section of the plan may be prepared."[24]

The descriptive handbook goes on to describe the drafting of an operations plan in the following terms:

"As the committee commences the drafting of a plan, it calls upon the experience and advice of the agencies chiefly responsible for its subsequent execution. And before the final draft is presented to the Board, interested diplomatic missions abroad are also asked to contribute or comment. Preparation of an operations plan helps to identify, clarify, and resolve differences of policy interpretation, operating responsibility, or required actions. It also exposes operating difficulties and recommends practical solutions for the more effective implementation of the policy." [25]

In the past 6 months, the Board has redesigned its operations plans so that they now consist entirely of general and detailed guidance. An annex to each plan describes each operating agency's programs.

After the interdepartmental working group has completed its draft of the plan, it must go to the Board assistants for further review and is then submitted to the Board itself for approval. Once approved, it represents the authoritative statement of what the particular National Security Council policy paper means in terms of more detailed and specific policy implications and implementing U.S. programs. The operations plans may be reviewed and modified at any time, but, until fairly recently, there was a requirement for formal review and revision every 6 months, and in addition, the Board was required to report to the National Security Council every 6 months indicating both progress and difficulties in the implementation of the various national security policies. The Board was also supposed to bring to the attention of the Council those policies which, in its view, required serious review and possibly modification.

This procedure has now been changed. The working groups must still evaluate both the operations plans and the policies underlying them every 6 months and then indicate to the Board whether new developments have arisen which require changes either in the plans or in the guiding policies. If either a review of or a change in the underlying policy is recommended to it, the Board must then decide whether the matter should be put before the Security Council. In

[24] Operations Coordinating Board, *op. cit.*, point 20.
[25] *Ibid.*, point 21.

other words, there has been an increase in the discretionary authority granted to the Board. In place of a requirement for periodic progress reports from the Board to the Council, the Board is now responsible for alerting the President and the National Security Council to those particular developments and situations that seem to call for the review of existing policy.

Thus, following the process which has brought a policy paper from the Planning Board stage to the National Security Council and then into the hands of the Operations Coordinating Board, the whole cycle may start again with an analysis by the Planning Board and the departmental units that support its activities, a request for a new national intelligence estimate on the subject, and eventually renewed discussion and consideration in the Council.

SPECIALIZED FUNCTIONS

7   *Intelligence*

The complexities of foreign policy in our day, and the extra-ordinarily high costs and risks that may attach to the slightest mis-take or misstep, have put a very high premium on adequate, accurate, and timely intelligence concerning the capabilities and intentions of our competitors in the international arena. A great deal thus hangs on the success or failure of men and institutions whose information-gathering work is normally hidden from public view. We rejoice in the spectacular successes, like the timely discovery of Soviet missile installations being built in Cuba in October 1962. And we occa-sionally pay the price of spectacular failures, like the Chinese inter-vention in the Korean war at the end of 1950, or, earlier, the Japanese attack on Pearl Harbor on December 7, 1941. In the following selec-tion, Roberta Wohlstetter reviews the nature of the "intelligence failure" at Pearl Harbor, clarifying some crucial human capacities in intelligence work that are as relevant today as they were twenty-five years ago.

Surprise

ROBERTA WOHLSTETTER

If our intelligence system and all our other channels of in-formation failed to produce an accurate image of Japanese inten-tions and capabilities, it was not for want of the relevant materials.

Reprinted from *Pearl Harbor: Warning and Decision,* by Roberta Wohlstetter, with the permission of the publishers, Stanford University Press. © 1962 by the Board of Trustees of the Leland Stanford Junior University.

111

Never before have we had so complete an intelligence picture of the enemy. And perhaps never again will we have such a magnificent collection of sources at our disposal.

RETROSPECT

To review these sources briefly, an American cryptanalyst, Col. William F. Friedman, had broken the top-priority Japanese diplomatic code, which enabled us to listen to a large proportion of the privileged communications between Tokyo and the major Japanese embassies throughout the world. Not only did we know in advance how the Japanese ambassadors in Washington were advised, and how much they were instructed to say, but we also were listening to top-secret messages on the Tokyo-Berlin and Tokyo-Rome circuits, which gave us information vital for conduct of the war in the Atlantic and Europe. In the Far East this source provided minute details on movements connected with the Japanese program of expansion into Southeast Asia.

Besides the strictly diplomatic codes, our cryptanalysts also had some success in reading codes used by Japanese agents in major American and foreign ports. Those who were on the distribution list for MAGIC* had access to much of what these agents were reporting to Tokyo and what Tokyo was demanding of them in the Panama Canal Zone, in cities along the east and west coasts of the Americas from northern Canada as far south as Brazil, and in ports throughout the Far East, including the Philippines and the Hawaiian Islands. They could determine what installations, what troop and ship movements, and what alert and defense measures were of interest to Tokyo at these points on the globe, as well as approximately how much correct information her agents were sending her.

Our naval leaders also had at their disposal the results of radio traffic analysis. While before the war our naval radio experts could not read the content of any Japanese naval or military coded messages, they were able to deduce from a study of intercepted ship call signs the composition and location of the Japanese Fleet units. After a change in call signs, they might lose sight of some units, and units that went into port in home waters were also lost because the ships in port used frequencies that our radios were unable to intercept. Most of the time, however, our traffic analysts had the various Japanese Fleet units accurately pinpointed on our naval maps.

* The intercepted diplomatic messages. — Ed.

Extremely competent on-the-spot economic and political analysis was furnished by Ambassador Grew and his staff in Tokyo. Ambassador Grew was himself a most sensitive and accurate observer, as evidenced by his dispatches to the State Department. His observations were supported and supplemented with military detail by frequent reports from American naval attachés and observers in key Far Eastern ports. Navy Intelligence had men with radio equipment located along the coast of China, for example, who reported the convoy movements toward Indochina. There were also naval observers stationed in various high-tension areas in Thailand and Indochina who could fill in the local outlines of Japanese political intrigue and military planning. In Tokyo and other Japanese cities, it is true, Japanese censorship grew more and more rigid during 1941, until Ambassador Grew felt it necessary to disclaim any responsibility for noting or reporting overt military evidence of an imminent outbreak of war. This careful Japanese censorship naturally cut down visual confirmation of the decoded information but very probably never achieved the opaqueness of Russia's Iron Curtain.

During this period the data and interpretations of British intelligence were also available to American officers in Washington and the Far East, though the British and Americans tended to distrust each other's privileged information.

In addition to secret sources, there were some excellent public ones. Foreign correspondents for *The New York Times, The Herald Tribune,* and *The Washington Post* were stationed in Tokyo and Shanghai and in Canberra, Australia. Their reporting as well as their predictions on the Japanese political scene were on a very high level. Frequently their access to news was more rapid and their judgment of its significance as reliable as that of our Intelligence officers. This was certainly the case for 1940 and most of 1941. For the last few weeks before the Pearl Harbor strike, however, the public newspaper accounts were not very useful. It was necessary to have secret information in order to know what was happening. Both Tokyo and Washington exercised very tight control over leaks during this crucial period, and the newsmen accordingly had to limit their accounts to speculation and notices of diplomatic meetings with no exact indication of the content of the diplomatic exchanges.

The Japanese press was another important public source. During

1941 it proclaimed with increasing shrillness the Japanese government's determination to pursue its program of expansion into Southeast Asia and the desire of the military to clear the Far East of British and American colonial exploitation. This particular source was rife with explicit signals of aggressive intent.

Finally, an essential part of the intelligence picture for 1941 was both public and privileged information on American policy and activities in the Far East. During the year the pattern of action and interaction between the Japanese and American governments grew more and more complex. At the last, it became especially important for anyone charged with the responsibility of ordering an alert to know what moves the American government was going to make with respect to Japan, as well as to try to guess what Japan's next move would be, since Japan's next move would respond in part to ours. Unfortunately our military leaders, and especially our Intelligence officers, were sometimes as surprised as the Japanese at the moves of the White House and the State Department. They usually had more orderly anticipations about Japanese policy and conduct than they had about America's. On the other hand, it was also true that State Department and White House officials were handicapped in judging Japanese intentions and estimates of risk by an inadequate picture of our own military vulnerability.

All of the public and private sources of information mentioned were available to America's political and military leaders in 1941. It is only fair to remark, however, that no single person or agency ever had at any given moment all the signals existing in this vast information network. The signals lay scattered in a number of different agencies; some were decoded, some were not; some traveled through rapid channels of communication, some were blocked by technical or procedural delays; some never reached a center of decision. But it is legitimate to review again the general sort of picture that emerged during the first week of December from the signals readily at hand. Anyone close to President Roosevelt was likely to have before him the following significant fragments.

There was first of all a picture of gathering troop and ship movements down the China coast and into Indochina. The large dimensions of this movement to the south were established publicly and visually as well as by analysis of ship call signs. Two changes in Japanese naval call signs — one on November 1 and another on December 1 — had also been evaluated by Naval Intelligence as extremely unusual and as signs of major preparations for some sort of Japanese offensive. The two changes had interfered with the speed of American radio traffic analysis. Thousands of interceptions after December 1 were necessary before the new call signs could be read. Partly for this reason American radio analysts disagreed about the locations of the Japanese carriers. One group held that all the carriers were near Japan because they had not been able to identify a carrier call sign since the middle of November. Another group believed that they had located one carrier division in the Marshalls. The probability seemed to be that the carriers, wherever they were, had gone into radio silence; and past experience led the analysts to believe that they were therefore in waters near the Japanese homeland, where they could communicate with each other on wavelengths that we could not intercept. However, our inability to locate the carriers exactly, combined with the two changes in call signs, was itself a danger signal.

Our best secret source, MAGIC, was confirming the aggressive intention of the new military cabinet in Tokyo, which had replaced the last moderate cabinet on October 17. In particular, MAGIC provided details of some of the preparations for the move into Southeast Asia. Running counter to this were increased troop shipments to the Manchurian border in October. (The intelligence picture is never clear-cut.) But withdrawals had begun toward the end of that month. MAGIC also carried explicit instructions to the Japanese ambassadors in Washington to pursue diplomatic negotiations with the United States with increasing energy, but at the same time it announced a deadline for the favorable conclusion of the negotiations, first for November 25, later postponed until November 29. In case of diplomatic failure by that date, the Japanese ambassadors were told, Japanese patience would be exhausted, Japan was determined to pursue her Greater East Asia policy, and on November 29 "things" would automatically begin to happen.

On November 26 Secretary Hull rejected Japan's latest bid for American approval of her policies in China and Indochina. MAGIC had repeatedly characterized this Japanese overture as the "last," and it now revealed the ambassadors' reaction of consternation and despair over the American refusal and also their country's characterization of the American Ten Point Note as an "ultimatum."

On the basis of this collection of signals, Army and Navy Intelligence experts in Washington tentatively placed D-day *for the Japa-*

nese Southeastern campaign during the week end of November 30, and when this failed to materialize, during the week end of December 7. They also compiled an accurate list of probable British and Dutch targets and included the Philippines and Guam as possible American targets.

Also available in this mass of information, but long forgotten, was a rumor reported by Ambassador Grew in January, 1941. It came from what was regarded as a not-very-reliable source, the Peruvian embassy, and stated that the Japanese were preparing a surprise air attack on Pearl Harbor. Curiously the date of the report is coincident roughly with what we now know to have been the date of inception of Yamamoto's plan; but the rumor was labeled by everyone, including Ambassador Grew, as quite fantastic and the plan as absurdly impossible. American judgment was consistent with Japanese judgment at this time, since Yamamoto's plan was in direct contradiction to Japanese naval tactical doctrine.

PERSPECTIVE

On the basis of this rapid recapitulation of the highlights in the signal picture, it is apparent that our decisionmakers had at hand an impressive amount of information on the enemy. They did not have the complete list of targets, since none of the last-minute estimates included Pearl Harbor. They did not know the exact hour and date for opening the attack. They did not have an accurate knowledge of Japanese capabilities or of Japanese ability to accept very high risks. The crucial question then, we repeat, is, If we could enumerate accurately the British and Dutch targets and give credence to a Japanese attack against them either on November 30 or December 7, why were we not expecting a specific danger to *ourselves?* And by the word "expecting," we mean expecting in the sense of taking specific alert actions to meet the contingencies of attack by land, sea, or air.

There are several answers to this question that have become apparent in the course of this study. First of all, it is much easier *after* the event to sort the relevant from the irrelevant signals. After the event, of course, a signal is always crystal clear; we can now see what disaster it was signaling, since the disaster has occurred. But before the event it is obscure and pregnant with conflicting meanings. It comes to the observer embedded in an atmosphere of "noise," i.e., in the company of all sorts of information that is useless and irrelevant for predicting the particular disaster. For example, in Washington, Pearl Harbor signals were competing with a vast number of signals from the European theater. These European signals announced danger more frequently and more specifically than any coming from the Far East. The Far Eastern signals were also arriving at a center of decision where they had to compete with the prevailing belief that an unprotected offensive force acts as a deterrent rather than a target. In Honolulu they were competing *not* with signals from the European theater, but rather with a large number of signals announcing Japanese intentions and preparations to attack Soviet Russia rather than to move southward; here they were also competing with expectations of local sabotage prepared by previous alert situations.

In short, we failed to anticipate Pearl Harbor not for want of the relevant materials, but because of a plethora of irrelevant ones. Much of the appearance of wanton neglect that emerged in various investigations of the disaster resulted from the unconscious suppression of vast congeries of signs pointing in every direction except Pearl Harbor. It was difficult later to recall these signs since they had led nowhere. Signals that are characterized today as absolutely unequivocal warnings of surprise air attack on Pearl Harbor become, on analysis in the context of December, 1941, not merely ambiguous but occasionally inconsistent with such an attack. To recall one of the most controversial and publicized examples, the winds code, both General Short and Admiral Kimmel testified that if they had had this information, they would have been prepared on the morning of December 7 for an air attack from without. The messages establishing the winds code are often described in the Pearl Harbor literature as Tokyo's declaration of war against America. If they indeed amounted to such a declaration, obviously the failure to inform Honolulu of this vital news would have been criminal negligence. On examination, however, the messages proved to be instructions for code communication after normal commercial channels had been cut. In one message the recipient was instructed on receipt of an execute to destroy all remaining codes in his possession. In another version the recipient was warned that the execute would be sent out "when relations are becoming dangerous" between Japan and three other countries. There was a different code term for each country: England, America, and the Soviet Union.

There is no evidence that an authentic execute of either message was ever intercepted by the United States before December 7. The message ordering code destruction was in any case superseded by a much more explicit code-destruction order from Tokyo that was intercepted on December 2 and translated on December 3. After December 2, the receipt of a winds-code execute for code destruction would therefore have added nothing new to our information, and code destruction in itself cannot be taken as an unambiguous substitute for a formal declaration of war. During the first week of December the United States ordered all American consulates in the Far East to destroy all American codes, yet no one has attempted to prove that this order was equivalent to an American declaration of war against Japan. As for the other winds-code message, provided an execute had been received warning that relations were dangerous between Japan and the United States, there would still have been no way on the basis of this signal alone to determine whether Tokyo was signaling Japanese intent to attack the United States or Japanese fear of an American surprise attack (in reprisal for Japanese aggressive moves against American allies in the Far East). It was only after the event that "dangerous relations" could be interpreted as "surprise air attack on Pearl Harbor."

There is a difference, then, between having a signal available somewhere in the heap of irrelevancies, and perceiving it as a warning; and there is also a difference between perceiving it as a warning, and acting or getting action on it. These distinctions, simple as they are, illuminate the obscurity shrouding this moment in history.

Many instances of these distinctions have been examined in the course of this study. We shall recall a few of the most dramatic now. To illustrate the difference between having and perceiving a signal, let us return to Colonel Fielder, whom we met in Chapter 1 [of the Wohlstetter book]. Though he was an untrained and inexperienced Intelligence officer, he headed Army Intelligence at Pearl Harbor at the time of the attack. He had been on the job for only four months, and he regarded as quite satisfactory his sources of information and his contacts with the Navy locally and with Army Intelligence in Washington. Evidently he was unaware that Army Intelligence in Washington was not allowed to send him any "action" or policy information, and he was therefore not especially concerned about trying to read beyond the obvious meaning of any given communication that came under his eyes. Colonel Bratton, head of Army Far Eastern Intelligence in Washington, however, had a somewhat more realistic view of the extent of Colonel Fielder's knowledge. At the end of November, Colonel Bratton had learned about the winds-code setup and was also apprised that the naval traffic analysis unit under Commander Rochefort in Honolulu was monitoring 24 hours a day for an execute. He was understandably worried about the lack of communication between this unit and Colonel Fielder's office, and by December 5 he finally felt that the matter was urgent enough to warrant sending a message directly to Colonel Fielder about the winds code. Now any information on the winds code, since it belonged to the highest classification of secret information, and since it was therefore automatically evaluated as "action" information, could not be sent through normal G-2 channels. Colonel Bratton had to figure out another way to get the information to Colonel Fielder. He sent this message: "Contact Commander Rochefort immediately thru Commandant Fourteenth Naval District regarding broadcasts from Tokyo reference weather." Signal Corps records establish that Colonel Fielder received this message. How did he react to it? He filed it. According to his testimony in 1945, it made no impression on him and he did not attempt to see Rochefort. He could not sense any urgency behind the lines because he was not expecting immediate trouble, and his expectations determined what he read. A warning signal was available to him, but he did not perceive it.

Colonel Fielder's lack of experience may make this example seem to be an exception. So let us recall the performance of Captain Wilkinson, the naval officer who headed the Office of Naval Intelligence in Washington in the fall of 1941 and who is unanimously acclaimed for a distinguished and brilliant career. His treatment of a now-famous Pearl Harbor signal does not sound much different in the telling. After the event, the signal in question was labeled "the bomb-plot message." It originated in Tokyo on September 24 and was sent to an agent in Honolulu. It requested the agent to divide Pearl Harbor into five areas and to make his future reports on ships in harbor with reference to those areas. Tokyo was especially interested in the locations of battleships, destroyers, and carriers, and also in any information on the anchoring of more than one ship at a single dock.

This message was decoded and translated on October 9 and shortly thereafter distributed to Army, Navy, and State Department recipients of MAGIC. Commander Kramer, a naval expert on MAGIC, had marked the message with an asterisk, signifying that he thought it to be of particular interest. But what was its interest? Both he and Wilkinson agreed that it illustrated the "nicety" of Japanese intelligence, the incredible zeal and efficiency with which they collected detail. The division into areas was interpreted as a device for shortening the reports. Admiral Stark was similarly impressed with Japanese efficiency, and no one felt it necessary to forward the message to Admiral Kimmel. No one read into it a specific danger to ships anchored in Pearl Harbor. At the time, this was a reasonable estimate, since somewhat similar requests for information were going to Japanese agents in Panama, Vancouver, Portland, San Diego, San Francisco, and other places. It should be observed, however, that the estimate was reasonable only on the basis of a very rough check on the quantity of espionage messages passing between Tokyo and these American ports. No one in Far Eastern Intelligence had subjected the messages to any more refined analysis. An observer assigned to such a job would have been able to record an increase in the frequency and specificity of Tokyo's requests concerning Manila and Pearl Harbor in the last weeks before the outbreak of war, and he would have noted that Tokyo was not displaying the same interest in other American ports. These observations, while not significant in isolation, might have been useful in the general signal picture.

There is no need, however, to confine our examples to Intelligence personnel. Indeed, the crucial areas where the signals failed to communicate a warning were in the operational branches of the armed services. Let us take Admiral Kimmel and his reaction to the information that the Japanese were destroying most of their codes in major Far Eastern consulates and also in London and Washington. Since the Pearl Harbor attack, this information has frequently been characterized by military experts who were not stationed in Honolulu as an "unmistakable tip-off." As Admiral Ingersoll explained at the congressional hearings, with the lucidity characteristic of statements after the event:

> If you rupture diplomatic negotiations you do not necessarily have to burn your codes. The diplomats go home and they can pack up their codes with their dolls and take them home. Also, when you rupture diplomatic negotiations, you do not rupture consular relations. The consuls stay on.
>
> Now, in this particular set of dispatches that did not mean a rupture of

diplomatic negotiations, it meant war, and that information was sent out to the fleets as soon as we got it. . . .[1]

The phrase "it meant war" was, of course, pretty vague; war in Manila, Hong Kong, Singapore, and Batavia is not war 5,000 miles away in Pearl Harbor. Before the event, for Admiral Kimmel, code burning in major Japanese consulates in the Far East may have "meant war," but it did not signal danger of an air attack on Pearl Harbor. In the first place, the information that he received was not the original MAGIC. He learned from Washington that Japanese consulates were burning "almost all" of their codes, not all of them, and Honolulu was not included on the list. He knew from a local source that the Japanese consulate in Honolulu was burning secret papers (not necessarily codes), and this back yard burning had happened three or four times during the year. In July, 1941, Kimmel had been informed that the Japanese consulates in lands neighboring Indochina had destroyed codes, and he interpreted the code burning in December as a similar attempt to protect codes in case the Americans or their British and Dutch allies tried to seize the consulates in reprisal for the southern advance. This also was a reasonable interpretation at the time, though not an especially keen one.

Indeed, at the time there was a good deal of evidence available to support all the wrong interpretations of last-minute signals, and the interpretations appeared wrong only *after* the event. There was, for example, a good deal of evidence to support the hypothesis that Japan would attack the Soviet Union from the east while the Russian Army was heavily engaged in the west. Admiral Turner, head of Navy War Plans in Washington, was an enthusiastic adherent of this view and argued the high probability of a Japanese attack on Russia up until the last week in November, when he had to concede that most of Japan's men and supplies were moving south. Richard Sorge, the expert Soviet spy who had direct access to the Japanese Cabinet, had correctly predicted the southern move as early as July, 1941, but even he was deeply alarmed during September and early October by the large number of troop movements to the Manchurian border. He feared that his July advice to the Soviet Union had been in error, and his alarm ultimately led to his capture on October 14. For at this time he increased his radio messages to Moscow to the

[1] *Hearings* [*before the Joint Committee on the Investigation of the Pearl Harbor Attack*], Part 9, p. 4226.

point where it was possible for the Japanese police to pinpoint the source of the broadcasts.

It is important to emphasize here that most of the men that we have cited in our examples, such as Captain Wilkinson and Admirals Turner and Kimmel — these men and their colleagues who were involved in the Pearl Harbor disaster — were as efficient and loyal a group of men as one could find. Some of them were exceptionally able and dedicated. The fact of surprise at Pearl Harbor has never been persuasively explained by accusing the participants, individually or in groups, of conspiracy or negligence or stupidity. What these examples illustrate is rather the very human tendency to pay attention to the signals that support current expectations about enemy behavior. If no one is listening for signals of an attack against a highly improbable target, then it is very difficult for the signals to be heard.

For every signal that came into the information net in 1941 there were usually several plausible alternative explanations, and it is not surprising that our observers and analysts were inclined to select the explanations that fitted the popular hypotheses. They sometimes set down new contradictory evidence side by side with existing hypotheses, and they also sometimes held two contradictory beliefs at the same time. We have seen this happen in G-2 estimates for the fall of 1941. Apparently human beings have a stubborn attachment to old beliefs and an equally stubborn resistance to new material that will upset them.

Besides the tendency to select whatever was in accord with one's expectations, there were many other blocks to perception that prevented our analysts from making the correct interpretation. We have just mentioned the masses of conflicting evidence that supported alternative and equally reasonable hypotheses. This is the phenomenon of noise in which a signal is embedded. Even at its normal level, noise presents problems in distraction; but in addition to the natural clatter of useless information and competing signals, in 1941 a number of factors combined to raise the usual noise level. First of all, it had been raised, especially in Honolulu, by the background of previous alert situations and false alarms. Earlier alerts, as we have seen, had centered attention on local sabotage and on signals supporting the hypothesis of a probable Japanese attack on Russia. Second, in both Honolulu and Washington, individual reactions to danger had been numbed, or at least dulled, by the continuous international tension.

A third factor that served to increase the natural noise level was the positive effort made by the enemy to keep the relevant signals quiet. The Japanese security system was an important and successful block to perception. It was able to keep the strictest cloak of secrecy around the Pearl Harbor attack and to limit knowledge only to those closely associated with the details of military and naval planning. In the Japanese Cabinet only the Navy Minister and the Army Minister (who was also Prime Minister) knew of the plan before the task force left its final port of departure.

In addition to keeping certain signals quiet, the enemy tried to create noise, and sent false signals into our information system by carrying on elaborate "spoofs." False radio traffic made us believe that certain ships were maneuvering near the mainland of Japan. The Japanese also sent to individual commanders false war plans for Chinese targets, which were changed only at the last moment to bring them into line with the Southeastern movement.

A fifth barrier to accurate perception was the fact that the relevant signals were subject to change, often very sudden change. This was true even of the so-called static intelligence, which included data on capabilities and the composition of military forces. In the case of our 1941 estimates of the infeasibility of torpedo attacks in the shallow waters of Pearl Harbor, or the underestimation of the range and performance of the Japanese Zero, the changes happened too quickly to appear in an intelligence estimate.

Sixth, our own security system sometimes prevented the communication of signals. It confronted our officers with the problem of trying to keep information from the enemy without keeping it from each other, and, as in the case of MAGIC, they were not always successful. As we have seen, only a very few key individuals saw these secret messages, and they saw them only briefly. They had no opportunity or time to make a critical review of the material, and each one assumed that others who had seen it would arrive at identical interpretations. Exactly who those "others" were was not quite clear to any recipient. Admiral Stark, for example, thought Admiral Kimmel was reading all of MAGIC. Those who were not on the list of recipients, but who had learned somehow of the existence of the decodes, were sure that they contained military as well as diplomatic information and believed that the contents were much fuller and more precise than they actually were. The effect of carefully limiting the reading and discussion of MAGIC, which was certainly necessary to safeguard the secret of our knowledge of the code, was thus to reduce this group of signals to the point where they were scarcely heard.

To these barriers of noise and security we must add the fact that the necessarily precarious character of intelligence information and predictions was reflected in the wording of instructions to take action. The warning messages were somewhat vague and ambiguous. Enemy moves are often subject to reversal on short notice, and this was true for the Japanese. They had plans for canceling their attacks on American possessions in the Pacific up to 24 hours before the time set for attack. A full alert in the Hawaiian Islands, for example, was one condition that might have caused the Pearl Harbor task force to return to Japan on December 5 or 6. The fact that intelligence predictions must be based on moves that are almost always reversible makes understandable the reluctance of the intelligence analyst to make bold assertions. Even if he is willing to risk his reputation on a firm prediction of attack at a definite time and place, no commander will in turn lightly risk the penalties and costs of a full alert. In December, 1941, a full alert required shooting down any unidentified aircraft sighted over the Hawaiian Islands. Yet this might have been interpreted by Japan as the first overt act. At least that was one consideration that influenced General Short to order his lowest degree of alert. While the cautious phrasing in the messages to the theater is certainly understandable, it nevertheless constituted another block on the road to perception. The sentences in the final theater warnings — "A surprise aggressive move in any direction is a possibility" and "Japanese future action unpredictable but hostile action possible at any moment" — could scarcely have been expected to inform the theater commanders of any change in their strategic situation.

Last but not least we must also mention the blocks to perception and communication inherent in any large bureaucratic organization, and those that stemmed from intraservice and interservice rivalries. The most glaring example of rivalry in the Pearl Harbor case was that between Naval War Plans and Naval Intelligence. A general prejudice against intellectuals and specialists, not confined to the military but unfortunately widely held in America, also made it difficult for intelligence experts to be heard. McCollum, Bratton,

Sadtler, and a few others who felt that the signal picture was ominous enough to warrant more urgent warnings had no power to influence decision. The Far Eastern code analysts, for example, were believed to be too immersed in the "Oriental point of view." Low budgets for American Intelligence departments reflected the low prestige of this activity, whereas in England, Germany, and Japan, 1941 budgets reached a height that was regarded by the American Congress as quite beyond reason.

❊   ❊   ❊   ❊   ❊

In view of all these limitations to perception and communication, is the fact of surprise at Pearl Harbor, then, really so surprising? Even with these limitations explicitly recognized, there remains the step between perception and action. Let us assume that the first hurdle has been crossed: An available signal has been perceived as an indication of imminent danger. Then how do we resolve the next questions: What specific danger is the signal trying to communicate, and what specific action or preparation should follow?

On November 27, General MacArthur had received a war warning very similar to the one received by General Short in Honolulu. MacArthur's response had been promptly translated into orders designed to protect his bombers from possible air attack from Formosan land bases. But the orders were carried out very slowly. By December 8, Philippine time, only half of the bombers ordered to the south had left the Manila area, and reconnaissance over Formosa had not been undertaken. There was no sense of urgency in preparing for a Japanese air attack, partly because our intelligence estimates had calculated that the Japanese aircraft did not have sufficient range to bomb Manila from Formosa.

The information that Pearl Harbor had been attacked arrived at Manila early in the morning of December 8, giving the Philippine forces some 9 or 10 hours to prepare for an attack. But did an air attack on Pearl Harbor necessarily mean that the Japanese would strike from the air at the Philippines? Did they have enough equipment to mount both air attacks successfully? Would they come from Formosa or from carriers? Intelligence had indicated that they would have to come from carriers, yet the carriers were evidently off Hawaii. MacArthur's headquarters also pointed out that there had been no formal declaration of war against Japan by the United

States. Therefore approval could not be granted for a counterattack on Formosan bases. Furthermore there were technical disagreements among airmen as to whether a counterattack should be mounted without advance photographic reconnaissance. While Brereton was arranging permission to undertake photographic reconnaissance, there was further disagreement about what to do with the aircraft in the meantime. Should they be sent aloft or should they be dispersed to avoid destruction in case the Japanese reached the airfields? When the Japanese bombers arrived shortly after noon, they found all the American aircraft wingtip to wingtip on the ground. Even the signal of an actual attack on Pearl Harbor was not an unambiguous signal of an attack on the Philippines, and it did not make clear what response was best.

8   Planning in Foreign Policy

In the conduct of foreign affairs, the present and the future are often in competition with each other. The Department of State can hardly help but be oriented toward the unfolding problems of contemporary foreign policy; this is its chief responsibility, and we measure its performance by the way it copes with these problems. But the Department also has to think systematically about the problems and the needs of tomorrow, or else it will be forever surprised by and unprepared for those developments that unfold each day. Out of the tug of war between the demands of the present and the future has emerged the concept of foreign policy planning; there has been a formal policy-planning office in the State Department since 1947. But an acceptance of the need for policy planning has made more acute the question, "What kind of planning?" or "Planning for what?" One conception of foreign policy planning is "contingency planning" — the systematic and inspired reading of the future and the advance preparation of policy responses for the most likely challenges. In practice, however, the future has held too many reasonable possibilities, problems have often emerged into the pres-

*ent rather differently than expected, and the planners themselves
have been drawn, by their own interests and by demands for their
skills, away from their speculations about the future into the policy
debates of the present. Against these almost inherent difficulties in
contingency planning, Franklin A. Lindsay proposes here a different kind of forward thinking and action.*

Program Planning: The Missing Element

FRANKLIN A. LINDSAY

I

It is now generally accepted that in the last 15 years the
conduct of our foreign affairs has undergone a fundamental revolution. The United States has progressed from an era in which foreign
policy was executed only through negotiations between an ambassador and a foreign minister to an era in which the broadest and
most active contacts are maintained at all levels within a foreign
country. In many areas of the world, we are actually helping to
build new nations from the ground up.

Before World War II, our concern with foreign affairs was much
more limited. The active issues of policy requiring foresighted planning were confined almost entirely to tariff and disarmament negotiations and these occasional activities could be handled by a small
corps of professional diplomats, aided by a few professional soldiers.
All that was required was: first, broad policy decisions on the positions to be taken; second, diplomatic negotiations with other interested powers; and possibly third, treaty ratifications if negotiations
were successful. This was the totality of foreign affairs. Even Sir
Harold Nicolson, in his classic book "Diplomacy," written in 1939,
treated diplomacy as the sole means available to a nation for the
peacetime execution of foreign policy.

Reprinted from Franklin A. Lindsay, "Program Planning: The Missing Element," *Foreign Affairs*, Vol. 39, No. 2, January 1961, pp. 279–90. Copyright
1960 by Council on Foreign Relations, Inc., New York.

In today's world, the tools for carrying out policy have multiplied. In addition to diplomacy, they include information and propaganda; economic aid; technical assistance; scientific discovery and development; educational and cultural activities; monetary, trade and tariff controls; foreign military assistance and the maintenance of military power in being. Under these circumstances, the conduct of foreign policy becomes incredibly more complex. Today 16 separate departments and agencies of government have a major concern with foreign affairs and 20 more have a somewhat lesser concern. Each of these organizations conducts its own programs, either directly or indirectly in contact with foreign governments and peoples. Each competes for limited resources of money, facilities and skilled manpower.

The need to coordinate these many activities has been seen since the end of World War II, and many proposals have been made to cope with it. But they have not dealt with a related problem which may be even more responsible for the many shortcomings now generally recognized in our foreign policy. The second weakness is the inadequacy of planning, or perhaps more precisely of program planning, at all levels of government.

Program planning is the process by which policy objectives are translated into action programs of the scope, magnitude, and timing required for their realization. Because today's policies require massive applications of manpower, money and facilities — and because it takes time to bring these assets into being — we must increasingly *anticipate* the needs posed by our objectives. It takes years to train a public information officer capable of working effectively in, say, Southeast Asia, to bring into being a new investment bank capable of wisely directing the flow of capital investment, to build a competent corps of public administrators in a newly developing country, or to create a limited-war military force capable of moving at a moment's notice by air to a distant point of danger. We are doing this job inadequately today because we are not anticipating sufficiently our needs for these instruments of policy execution. Hence our foreign policy often must be "reactive" simply because we have not created in advance the assets needed to take the initiative.

Last fall, for example, the Government asked for outside assistance in recruiting from private life no less than 15 financial advisers for 15 new countries, mostly in Africa. The sudden requirement was the result of a failure to foresee this need and to train a corps of financial advisers who were competent to deal both with the technical and with the political problems of underdeveloped nations. The jobs had been open for several months, and at that time there had been no success in filling them. When a likely candidate is found who is reasonably competent professionally, he undoubtedly will be shipped off to Africa immediately. But he almost certainly will not have had any special training in the economics, politics or social structure of the country to which he is assigned. And this lack of background will hamper his effectiveness as a financial adviser, as well as his ability to help prepare the country to mature politically within the free world.

This is not an isolated case of lack of planning. None of the principal agencies of government concerned with foreign affairs foresaw the emergence of new independent states in Africa even to the extent of starting special training programs for their own career personnel. As a result, posts in Africa are either entirely unmanned or filled by officers hastily reassigned from other areas of the world, and by new recruits fresh out of college.

In the field of disarmament the record of the last 15 years is largely of one makeshift improvisation after another. In April 1958, for example, the President proposed to the Soviets that a conference of technicians be convened to consider the problems of preventing surprise attack. On September 15 the Soviets accepted the proposal and asked that the conference begin on November 10. As of the date of Soviet acceptance, almost no preparations had been made, and it was not until October 2, when William C. Foster was appointed chairman, that work began on the preparation of policy positions. Groups were hastily assembled, both from within and outside government, to work for the remaining month before the conference. At the end of the conference, which reached no agreement, Mr. Foster reported to the Senate, "I doubt that we have up to this time really given the intense study of the kinds of measures which will make the [prevention of surprise attack] possible . . . I think that with hard work and deep thought and putting together competent people to work on this, not on a part-time basis but on a full-time basis, something very valuable could be accomplished."

Again in 1959 the same thing happened. In January, the United States proposed that a group of qualified scientists be convened to study the technical possibilities of detecting underground tests. The Russians delayed for nearly a year and then announced that they were ready to meet immediately. A scientific team under Dr. James Fisk, President of the Bell Laboratories, was assembled and departed almost immediately for Geneva. Most of the preparations were carried out in Geneva concurrently with the negotiations. At this conference, agreement was reached that it would be possible to detect underground explosions above 5 kilotons with 160–170 seismic stations located throughout the world. Only later did we discover that perhaps ten times this number of stations would be required to achieve a reasonable probability of detection. This predicament was the result of inadequate planning and of inadequate research to back it up. Had an agreement been reached on the basis of the technical report, we could have found ourselves in the position of having either to live with an inadequate agreement or to suffer the political and propaganda consequences of abrogating the treaty.

II

The lack of program planning in the foreign field probably can be laid to two underlying causes: (1) skepticism about the value of planning — owing at least partly to a misconception of its role — on the part of many career Foreign Service officers; and (2) the inevitable operational orientation of most of the top foreign policy officials.

The essential unpredictability of the future is often used as the principal argument for not planning. A Foreign Service career officer, when asked why the State Department did not put more emphasis on planning, replied, "How can you plan foreign policy when no one can possibly know what Castro is going to do two years, or even two days, from now?"

This of course is a distortion of the purpose of planning. The purpose is not to prepare rigid programs that will apply only if predictions about future events have been accurate to the point of clairvoyance. Rather, the purpose is to prepare broad, flexible programs with room for manoeuvring as events take shape. One need not have been able to predict the revolt of the *Force Publique* in the Congo to foresee that there would be serious political instability and that political officers would be needed who were thoroughly acquainted with the forces at work there and who had, by their personal knowledge and acquaintanceship, covered all reasonable political bets, including both those who did and those who did not attain power.

Perhaps the skepticism with which some in the State Department regard planning stems from the career officer's traditional concept of diplomatic negotiation as the sharp cutting edge of foreign policy. Success as a diplomat is the ultimate in career success and usually is rewarded with assignment to the highest posts in the service. Diplomacy is an art that should by no means be depreciated, and we shall have great need for this skill over the years ahead, no matter how well we plan. But skill in diplomacy depends on an approach to problems that is quite different from that of a good planner. The diplomat must be able to make the best of day-to-day developments over which he has little or no control. The planner, in contrast, must try to anticipate future situations by building capabilities in advance to meet them.

A second reason for the lack of planning is that agency and departmental chiefs are forced by circumstance to devote practically all of their energies to operating problems. This is because the operating problems are the hot issues that demand immediate attention. They are played up in the press and are the subject of Congressional inquiries. They are the subject of urgent messages from foreign governments demanding immediate telegraphic replies. They are the latest bombshells of Khrushchev and Mao that require immediate attention. Planning, in contrast, has no day-to-day deadlines. Nor does planning bring immediate rewards. No one will know until years later whether or not a given plan has been adequate.

Even if there were no pressures of operating problems, the incentive to plan far in advance would be weak. The creation of the modern tools of foreign policy — whether they be technical systems for the verification of arms-control agreements or a corps of professionals skilled in nation building — often requires years of planning and preparation. A particular administration in Washington is thus dependent almost entirely on the assets that have been created by previous administrations and must make the best of it when these assets are inadequate to do the jobs at hand. Equally, the effort of any administration to plan and build new instruments of national power is a form of investment that will pay most of its dividends in subsequent administrations. For this reason the planning processes require greater institutionalization to ensure that future interests are not neglected by those who may never themselves enjoy the fruits of their planning.

Whatever the underlying causes of the lack of planning may be, however, the immediate cause is an inadequate organization for planning, both in the National Security Council and in the various departments having foreign policy interests. It is true that "planning bodies" exist. The NSC has a Planning Board, and the State Department has since 1950 had its own Policy Planning Staff, now headed by an Assistant Secretary reporting directly to the Secretary of State. Under the NSC there is also the Operations Coordinating Board, which is charged with coordinating the operational planning of the responsible agencies in their execution of NSC policies.

The titles of these three organizations suggest that the planning function is adequately recognized, in both the White House and the State Department. Unfortunately titles are often misleading, and that is true here. The Planning Staff of the NSC plans only in the sense that it prepares the groundwork of the NSC. It is composed of the deputies of the NSC representatives, and its function is to steer first drafts of national security policy statements through the shoals of interdepartmental interests. It is thus no more concerned with actual program planning than is its parent body, whose function is to establish national policies. These policies are, of necessity, broad and general statements of the problems confronting us, and of our objectives in coping with them. Moreover, the NSC is more concerned with short-range than with long-range problems.

A hypothetical NSC policy dealing with an underdeveloped country in which we are strongly interested might read something like this: "It shall be the policy of the United States to assist Country X in establishing a stable and effective government capable of maintaining public support, of progressing in a sustained and orderly manner with economic and social development, and of avoiding the extremes of Communism or right-wing dictatorship. The United States should be prepared to assist in improving public administration, in fostering economic development, and in upgrading general education."

Before approving a policy of this sort, the Council should be provided with a reasonably accurate estimate of the magnitude of the program that must be undertaken, the time required and the costs involved if the proposed policy is to have a reasonable chance of success. For without such an estimate, the Council cannot properly weigh the costs and urgency of implementing this program against the costs and urgency of implementing other programs in other areas.

Admittedly, many of the NSC policy papers do carry financial appendices that purport to be the price tags of the policies advocated. But these projections usually are not backed up by specific plans and hence do not accurately reflect the actual costs of the program if it were carried through in the magnitude needed to achieve the stated objective. More often these financial projections are based on last year's budget, increased or lowered by 5 or 10 per cent, depending on the shift in the urgency of the problem. This lack of adequate plans for arriving at the real cost of any individual program affects our total foreign policy. For without such information, the Executive Branch and the Congress cannot make informed decisions on the total amount of resources that should be allocated to foreign policy objectives, or on the division of these resources among competing programs.

The real decisions controlling the size and direction of foreign programs — and therefore many of the real decisions on basic policy — are made instead as a part of the annual budget process. In theory, the budget is expected to reflect and implement national security policies. In practice, these are so broadly drawn that a correspondingly broad range of alternative budgets can be accommodated. Because of the lack of adequate plans to implement these policies — and thereby to define more closely the dollar costs — the budgets can often be jiggered substantially in support of any one program at the expense of others. The result is that the budget sets the real scope of a program, and the plans — such as they are — are then made to fit that budget.

The budget-making process may even set the direction of a program. Since that process is an affair largely between the agency concerned, such as ICA, and the Appropriations Committees of Congress, with the Bureau of the Budget looking in to be sure that an over-all ceiling is not exceeded, there is no direct control to see that budgets reflect NSC policies. Further, the Committees of Congress are not privy to National Security Council policy documents, and it is highly doubtful that they would consider themselves bound by them in any case.

In the State Department, the Policy Planning Staff performs an important planning function — but it does only a small part of what is needed. Essentially the role of the Policy Planning Staff is to prepare papers from time to time on important problems over the horizon. The purpose of these papers is to call the Government's attention to a particularly serious situation that might be overlooked by those concentrating on a particular area or country. The staff considers its work done when it has flagged for attention such a newly emerging problem.

The other operating departments concerned with foreign affairs have limited program-planning activities. And nearly all of their efforts are similarly directed to the preparation of the annual budget. As a consequence, planning is largely limited to one-year periods. Once a budget is approved and funds provided, individual expenditures, other than regular and continuing expenses for such things as staff salaries, are approved primarily on a project-by-project basis. While the Operations Coordinating Board has responsibility for coordinating the operational planning of the departments, it lacks authority to direct such planning, it lacks an adequate staff, and it cannot concern itself with any problem that has not been specifically referred to it by the President.

Some progress is being made toward better coordination of some of the Government's activities in the foreign field. As a result of the recommendations of the Draper Committee, the State Department now approves all military aid programs to foreign nations. Also, Under Secretary of State Douglas Dillon has begun to coordinate economic aid programs and to assemble a staff for this work. And in our embassies abroad, there has gradually evolved the concept of a country team headed by the Ambassador and including heads of the local information, economic and military-aid staffs.

These developments help to create a framework in which planning can take place. But coordination is still largely in terms of day-to-day operating decisions and such planning as is done is geared to yearly, and therefore short-term, budgets. These plans are thus more likely to be concerned with policies and programs for the use of assets already in being rather than with the estimation of over-all future needs and with the development of new programs to meet these needs. Moreover, the Government's over-all effort in one country or area is not examined as a single program so that the activities of the many separate agencies can all be evaluated for their completeness and balance. Instead, they are approved in small pieces over the year by a variety of agencies acting with only limited knowledge of each other's decisions.

In summary, without a clear-cut and generally understood plan bringing together the programs required in each of the essential fields of activity, the President and the Secretary of State cannot be sure that the responsible departments and agencies will start their programs soon enough or provide the magnitude of effort that is needed to realize objectives. Indeed, the record in many areas of the world is that of being too late and providing too little of those things that are vital to the success of our policies. To improve this record it will be necessary not only to revise our concept of planning, but to draw into the Government men with the background and experience to make planning effective.

We are confronted with formidable adversaries in the Soviet Union and Red China. While we should not embrace a tool of the cold war just because the Communists do, we should not deny ourselves such a tool because the Communists do use it effectively. Planning is a tool they appear to employ to great advantage. For example, one cannot imagine the Soviets finding it impossible to fill 15 jobs of financial adviser to foreign governments. They would not only be able to provide technicians competent to advise new governments in the Soviet approach to financial management, but those selected would be persuasive political advocates of the advantages of the Soviet system to the underdeveloped countries.

The Communists have demonstrated their ability to foresee future problems and opportunities and to plan well in advance to meet them. They have, for example, operated university-type training schools for potential political leaders of virtually all the uncommitted countries. In 1945, when they reinstituted these political academies, they did not know when Africa — or Southeast Asia — would be ready for a stepped-up program of political action. But they went ahead with comprehensive training programs with confidence that they would find the opportunity, sooner or later, to throw their trained cadres into the conflict.

III

To illustrate the type of planning needed, let us look again at the hypothetical NSC policy for Country X, which called for assistance "in establishing a stable and effective government . . . in improving public administration, in fostering economic development, and in upgrading general education." In developing a government-wide program plan to carry out that policy, the following sequence of steps might be taken.

1. Preparation of a preliminary estimate of what will be needed to establish a stable and effective non-Communist government. This

estimate must first identify those key needs that must be met if our policy objective is to be realized. In this example, the key needs might be a corps of public administrators, a police and public security force, public information media, and a program for economic growth. This estimate would include such things as numbers and types of skilled administrators needed; the investment requirements for economic growth; the needs for public information through books, magazines, radio, newspapers; the requirements for technicians and skilled workers; and the police forces needed to maintain order. Planning should then concentrate only on these key elements for "success" and should not be encumbered with nonessentials.

As a result of experience gained by American advisory groups who have served in underdeveloped countries, such as that to Pakistan headed by Professor Edward Mason of Harvard, we now have the resources in the United States to enable us to make reasonably accurate estimates of the initial critical needs in building a new nation.

2. An estimate of the degree to which these essential requirements can be met from the resources already available within the country. This would include personnel trained by the former government, European technicians and administrators likely to remain, and the graduates of technical and professional schools within the country and abroad.

3. An estimate of the remaining needs that must be met by the West if the minimum objectives are to have a reasonable chance of success. A part of these needs may be met by other nations, by the World Bank and possibly by the United Nations. The remaining critical needs will have to be provided by the United States.

4. At this point a preliminary estimate of costs and time required will provide a test of the feasibility of achieving the NSC policy objective. If it appears that requirements are substantially beyond our capabilities in the light of our resources and of other competing requirements, two alternatives are open: to shift resources from other programs or to cut back our policy objectives. If the latter is decided, an important function will have been served by putting ourselves on notice that actual or implied commitments to foreign governments beyond our limited resources must not be made.

5. A next step is the development by the responsible departments and agencies of more detailed but still long-term plans. For exam-

ple, the need for public administrators in the African countries may be so great that a major program must be established to create new institutes of public administration in Africa in addition to bringing increased numbers of Africans to the United States and Western Europe for further training. If a country has only 15 or 20 college graduates, as is actually the case in some of the new African republics, it will not be enough to spend a few thousand dollars — as we are, in some cases, doing now — to send an expert in public administration to the country or to bring a half dozen people to the United States for a limited period of training. While such a program might meet the letter of an NSC policy, it would not contribute very much to the solution of the problem. Similarly, the need for public information media may be so urgent — and the dangers of Communist infiltration and control so great — that USIA would be called upon to develop a program by which the Africans can be helped to set up locally-owned radio stations, a news agency, one or more book publishing houses and a series of newspapers.

The special importance of the planning process is that it provides an estimate of the magnitude of a problem early enough to do something about it. If instead we wait until the problem is breaking around our heads, it may be too late.

6. At this point planning should be tied integrally with the budget-making process. This will require a shift from the annual budget to longer-range commitments of funds. The approval of the policy program by the NSC and the approval of the budget to be submitted to Congress must be part of a single, consistent process. The present practice of preparing budgets only incidentally related to policy decisions clearly leads to breakdowns in the execution of policy.

7. Continuing central guidance and coordination of planning will be needed to be sure that the programs will be mutually supporting, and in the aggregate will give the best chance of success while making the minimum drain on scarce resources. Revision, modification and extension of plans will be a continuing process as new situations unfold and as we learn from initial successes and failures. Finally, at each step of the way we must work in close association with our allies, especially in those areas where they have important interests.

As the cold war develops during the 1960's, we must be increasingly prepared to seize opportunities as they occur. This means that we must think through in advance both the types of opportunities that might reasonably be expected and the actions we will have to take if we are not to let them slip by unexploited. By so doing we can create in advance assets that will be available when needed. For example, revolts such as those in East Germany and Hungary may occur in the next decade. If we fail to anticipate the different ways that events might unfold and to evaluate both the risks and opportunities of any action we might take, we will not know what preparations must be made in advance. If no preparations are made, there probably will be little or no freedom of decision at the moment the event occurs. As was the case in 1956, we shall have foregone the opportunity to exploit the break because we have not prepared for it. If, instead, we have made reasonably adequate contingency plans and have the necessary assets on hand, such as trained manpower, food, communications, medicines, air transport and weapons, we shall be free to decide at the time whether and to what degree we should intervene.

Obviously we cannot make plans for every conceivable contingency. Judgment must be used in identifying those possibilities that contain the greatest opportunities and dangers. Equally we cannot create assets to meet every contingency, but it is often possible to create assets that can be used in a variety of ways. A final question is, how shall comprehensive planning be organized? To this decision, the following criteria should be applied:

1. Centralized over-all direction and supervision of planning, to ensure completeness, balance and timeliness.

2. Decentralization of detailed planning, to ensure that plans are grounded in reality.

3. Full-time attention to planning by a small but highly competent group.

4. Accurate estimates of costs as plans are made, to provide adequate bases for budget decisions.

5. Follow-up and review, to ensure that plans are in fact carried out.

Clearly, to meet these criteria, a central planning staff will be needed. Its function will be to provide continuing leadership within the Government in the field of planning, to prepare over-all plans, to allocate responsibility for more detailed plans to departments and agencies, to review the adequacy of their plans and to see that approved plans are carried out. In all the operating departments and agencies, it should have small counterparts reporting directly to their agency heads but having day-to-day working contacts with responsible line officers, as well as with the central planning staff.

Many pieces of such a program already exist. What is lacking is central coordination and direction, and a philosophy to make it work. Through improved planning, we can significantly increase the probabilities that our foreign policies will be successful and that the vast resources we are now committing to these policies will be effectively used. Without it, there will be lost opportunities, half-effective programs and waste of resources. Program planning is not a strait jacket that commits us to a particular course of action, no matter what new circumstances arise, but a means of increasing our freedom of action and our ability to grasp the initiative in the long, cold war.

9   *Expert Advice: The Scientist as Policy Adviser*

Scientists have had an important voice in national security affairs since the advent of nuclear weapons in 1945. Many of the men who developed and refined the atomic and thermonuclear weapons stayed on, as it were, to try to exercise some influence over the possible uses and possible control of these devices. As the bearers of an extraordinary set of skills, they have asserted a special competence to deploy, in the interests of peace and security, the instruments they have created. But these scientists have not always agreed among themselves, nor have they had unchallenged possession of the title of expert. Over these two decades a number of nonscientist civilian specialists in military policy matters have appeared in government-supported research institutions like the RAND Corporation and subsequently in universities; their books and articles on national security policy have had an immense influence in shaping private and public thinking about these matters. We have already seen, in an earlier selection, an example of a scientist engaged

*in policy advice; in that instance Dr. Teller's arguments against the
nuclear test ban treaty, while heard with respect, were overridden.
In the following selection Albert Wohlstetter makes a direct assault
on the ardent claims of physical scientists for a preeminent role in
national security policy-making.*

Scientists, Seers and Strategy

ALBERT WOHLSTETTER

I

That scientists today crucially affect decisions on national
and international security — and therefore the fate of us all — will
come as no news. After radar and jets and the A-bomb and the
H-bomb and intercontinental rockets, the statement surely is obvious enough. But what does it mean? Like much else that is obvious, it is not very clear. Just how do the results of scientific research
and the methods of science and the scientists themselves actually
figure in decisions on arms and arms control? And how is the role of
the scientist in such matters related to the more familiar functions
of the politician, the military man and the ordinary citizen? Above
all, what does "scientist" mean in such statements?

Even partial answers to these hard questions might help us deal
with some others that are even harder and trouble us more. If by
"science" is meant a difficult and specialized discipline currently
accessible only to the few, a trained minority, what does this do to
the democratic process? At the end of his term in office, President
Eisenhower spoke of the danger that "public policy could itself
become the captive of a scientific-technological élite." On the other
hand, scientists, it seems, might become the captives. When scientists are drawn into the pulling and hauling of "politics," what hap-

Reprinted from Albert Wohlstetter, "Scientists, Seers and Strategy," *Foreign
Affairs*, Vol. 41, No. 3, April 1963, pp. 466–78. Copyright 1963 by Council
on Foreign Relations, Inc., New York.

This article is based on a longer monograph bearing the same title, presented
at a conference of the Council of Atomic Age Studies at Columbia University,
of which Mr. Christopher Wright is executive director.

pens to the freedom and objectivity of science or scientists? Again, given the partially hostile world in which we live, defense decisions must sometimes be made in secret. Where scientists are involved in such decisions, what does this mean for the vital features of science as a fallible but open, verifiable and self-correcting enterprise?

Especially in the two years or so since Sir Charles Snow's God-kin Lectures, discussion of these and related issues has been intense, sometimes bitter, and I think on the whole useful. But the issues have provided matter for both of Sir Charles' renowned "Two Cultures": exciting literary material and a supply of blunt weapons for the factional quarrels and feuds among scientists. As a result, while there has been some light shed, there has also been much mystification.

The Godkin Lectures, delivered at Harvard in the fall of 1960, begin with the dark words:

> One of the most bizarre features of any advanced industrial society in our time is that the cardinal choices have to be made by a handful of men: in secret: and, at least in legal form, by men who cannot have a first-hand knowledge of what those choices depend upon or what their results may be.
> When I say "advanced industrial society" I am thinking in the first place of the three in which I am most interested—the United States, the Soviet Union, and my own country. And when I say the "cardinal choices," I mean those which determine in the crudest sense whether we live or die.[1]

This opening sets C. P. Snow's major theme. He illustrated it, of course, with a dramatic story of the two English scientists, Sir Henry Tizard and F. A. Lindemann, Lord Cherwell, and their role in relation to the vital decisions on air defense and strategic bombing in England just before and during World War II.

If Sir Charles is right, the cardinal choices of the United States, the United Kingdom and the Soviet Union can, it seems, be directly understood only by scientists and yet are and must be, "at least in legal form," made by non-scientists who are exposed to the advice of only a few. Sir Charles, who is at home in both the Scientific Culture and the Literary one, moves so easily from one to the other that we are never quite sure how to take lessons from what he calls his "cautionary" tales. Are they literally true? Or are they literature?

---

[1] C. P. Snow, *Science and Government: The Godkin Lectures at Harvard, 1960* (Cambridge: Harvard University Press, 1961), p. 1.

The critical response to the Godkin Lectures by less partisan participants in the events they describe suggests that these stories may be
fables. None the less, even a fable may contain a useful moral: the
troubling questions remain.

In the limited sense of Snow's definition of "scientists," the cardinal choices referred to by Snow are not simply, as he suggests, a
domain of "science." The decision at the start of World War II to
develop a fission bomb, or the decision to use it against Japan, or the
decision to develop an H-bomb, or to bomb German cities during
World War II, called for much more than natural science and engineering. Such decisions have narrowly technological components,
but they involve just as essentially a great many other elements:
military operations and counter-operations by an enemy, the economics of industrial production, the social and political effects of
bombing on populations, and many others. Some of these other factors are qualitative. Many are quantitative, and in this very broad
sense "technical." (They involve numbers and may be related in a
numerical model.) However, even these do not fit into any of the
traditional disciplines of natural science or engineering. They do
not, for example, come under the head of electrical engineering or
physical chemistry. And natural scientists and engineers do not
normally acquire a professional acquaintance with subjects such as
the cost of buying and operating a fighter bomber or the disaster
behavior of urban populations. Nor do they ordinarily find these
subjects essential in the course of engineering work in developing a
bomb.

In fact, in addressing the complex cardinal choices, one of the
inadequacies sometimes displayed by natural scientists is that they
may ignore, or assume implicitly, or simply receive, or themselves
casually estimate without enough study, the values of those variables that fall outside the traditional natural science disciplines. The
cardinal choices, in Snow's sense, cannot be well made solely on
estimates of the feasibility or infeasibility of some piece of hard-
ware. They are political and military, strategic decisions. Technology is an important part, but very far from the whole of strategy.

Snow is not alone in creating this confusion. It is a very widespread practice among scientists concerned with public policy, and
especially among those who direct urgent popular appeals. In the
letter that Bertrand Russell sent in 1955 to heads of state enclosing
a call for what later became the Pugwash Conferences, he began:
"I enclose a statement, signed by some of the most eminent scien-

tific authorities on nuclear warfare." The signers were indeed without exception eminent scientists, but among the ten physicists, chemists and a mathematical logician who were included, not one to my knowledge had done any empirical study of military operations likely in a nuclear war.

Similarly it is usual to find, at the head of petitions advocating some specific nuclear policy, sentences that run: "As scientists we have knowledge of the dangers involved," followed by the signatures of tens or even thousands of scientists, only a few of whom have examined the empirical evidence on more than one or two of the many alternative dangers involved in the policy choice. Simply as a scientist no one has a knowledge of these complex choices.

The bombing controversy in 1942, one of the "cardinal choices" recounted by Snow, was somewhat ill-defined, as is not unusual in such policy disputes. It had to do among other matters with the relative emphasis in air strategy on offense or defense — with how, for example, to allocate resources between the strategic bombing of German towns and the air defense of coastal shipping. This is hardly the sort of thing one would normally submit to a vote of the Fellows of the Royal Society, as Snow suggests, or to the "general population" of natural scientists and engineers. And not simply or in principle because of the difficulties of secrecy.

A good answer to the allocation question depended on a great many things, including, on the one hand, how rapidly bombers would be manufactured, how soon after manufacture they could be made an operational part of the military forces, losses that might be expected from enemy defenses, the expected number of sorties in the operational life of these bombers, the shape and population density of German cities, and the types of building in them, the efficiency of the German fire-fighting services, the reaction of populations to the stress of air raids; and, on the other hand, the effectiveness of these same bombers against enemy ships of war, the allied shipping and supplies likely to be saved, the military worth of these supplies, etc., etc. These are not matters found in physics textbooks. Nor could the Fellows of the Royal Society be expected to qualify for independent judgment on them in the course of a week.

Over a longer period, such questions are open to study, but — and this is a critical point — they are open to study and answer by a much wider group than engineers and natural scientists. And there is little evidence to suggest that at such study the technologists are signally best. Not only are some of the principal variables subject matter for the behavioral sciences rather than physics, but the appropriate methods of study also may be closer to the methods of some behavioral sciences. Blackett, writing in 1943, not long after the bombing controversy, pointed out that the mathematical methods he employed are in general use

. . . in those branches of science whose subject matter has similar characteristics. These characteristics are that a limited amount of numerical data is ascertainable about phenomena of great complexity. The problems of analyzing war operations are almost all of this type and are therefore rather nearer, in general, to many problems, say, of biology or of economics, than to most problems of physics, where usually a great deal of numerical data is ascertainable about relatively simple phenomena.[2]

Perhaps even more important, while the job of gathering and examining relevant empirical data might be very laborious, the gist of the methods for using the data is quite generally accessible. The methods are within the grasp of an intelligent administrator, and, *given time,* open to his skeptical questioning.

I have stressed the phrase "given time." Without time on these complex questions, a government official is not likely to have a full understanding and may make some poor choices. This is also true, however, of the technologist or the analyst of tactics or strategies. One of the principal differences between our present situation and the circumstances in which decisions had to be made in World War II is that today we frequently have time. It is a salient difference bearing on the question of how technologists, strategists, military and political men may figure in cardinal choices. For the major peacetime decisions are seldom final. In short, given time, the decision-maker without a degree in physics, mathematics, or for that matter, mathematical economics, is quite capable of having a "first-hand knowledge of what those choices depend upon and what their result might be." [3] And he often will *have* time.

II

In the view of some scientists, it would appear that judgment does not really require time or a great deal of grubby work. It is, according to Snow, more a matter of intuition, an attribute of a few gifted

[2] "Operational Research," British Association for the Advancement of Science, Burlington House, Piccadilly, London. Reprinted from *The Advancement of Science,* Vol. 5, April 1948, p. 29 (Quarterly Journal of the British Association).

[3] *Science and Government,* p. 1.

men, a kind of "prescience." This quality evidently is present especially in scientists, who "have something to give which our kind of
existential society is desperately short of: so short of, that it fails to
recognise of what it is starved. That is foresight."[4] Foresight is "not
quite knowledge," but "much more an expectation of knowledge to
come . . . something that a scientist, if he has this kind of sensitivity latent in him, picks up during his scientific experience." [5] Some
men other than natural scientists have this gift but, we gather, much
more rarely and in a lesser degree.

The popular fantasies relating the pursuits of science to sorcery
and an almost superhuman thaumaturgy make such a view of prescience rather widely credible. Not only may the layman talk in
these terms of the mysteries of science, but also statesmen; the
"Wizard War" Churchill called the technological race in World
War II. We may not, as Mr. Eisenhower fears, become captive of a
scientific élite, but it would seem that scientists, or at least the best
scientists, may indeed be The Elect. And many of them have felt
charged with a prodigious mission and a great moral urgency.
Spurred by an apocalyptic vision of world annihilation, they urge a
drastic transformation in the conduct of world affairs in the immediate future. They have been passionately sure that the choices
are stark and clear: annihilation on the one hand or a paradise on
earth. "Remember your humanity and forget the rest," read the
invitation to the first Pugwash Conference. "If you can do so, the
way lies open to a new Paradise; if you cannot, there lies before
you the risk of universal death."

For many scientists there is very little time. C. P. Snow predicted
at the end of 1960 that if events proceed on their present course,
nuclear war is "a certainty . . . within at the most ten years." [6]
Which does not leave much time. The clock on the cover of the
Bulletin of the Atomic Scientists started so near twelve that a while
ago it had to be set back.

In bringing about a new sort of world, the scientists feel that they
have a special responsibility. They are free of the insincerities and
dubious motives of the traditional actors on the political scene; they

[4] *Ibid.*, p. 81.
[5] *Ibid.*, p. 82.
[6] "The Moral Un-Neutrality of Science," Address to the 1960 meeting of the
American Association for the Advancement of Science, reprinted in *Science*,
Jan. 27, 1961, Vol. 133, p. 259.

are interested only in clarification and truth. Furthermore the co-operative and potentially universal nature of the scientific enterprise is at hand as a model for a future world order, and the scientists can be vital agents in bringing that order about. "Scientists of the World, Unite!", the title of an article by a Princeton physicist appearing immediately after the war, sounds the right note.

This vision of the responsibility of the scientist — "a greater responsibility than is pressing on any other body of men,"[7] according to Snow — puts him in a very different role from the scientist as technologist or the scientist dealing by tentative and empirical methods with broader questions or cardinal choices. It is fortified, however, by the confusion between technologist and strategist and by the related notion of the scientist as specially endowed — a seer or prophet.

The notion bears a strange resemblance to that of the prophets in the chiliastic and apocalyptic movements that swept Europe centuries ago in times of great disorientation, anxiety and instability. It has some inspirational uses, but a great many disabilities. Like past eschatology, it encourages schismatics, and the feuds among the scientists have been intolerant and implicitly rather bloody. Snow's tale of Lindemann and Tizard unconsciously illustrates the point: Lindemann is the dark angel, sadistic and violent, without the gift of foresight. And Blackett, a passionate battler against the forces of darkness, uses the story in his innumerable present feuds.

But most important, this urgent, tense feeling of mission can sometimes bias the technological studies and, even more, tends to discourage the use of the patient and tentative method of science, as distinct from the *authority* of science, in assisting the cardinal choices of which Snow speaks. It has led in some cases to a rather surprising anti-rationalism.

III

Anyone who had searched diligently for a device, which in hostile hands might demolish what he had been building the previous year, is not likely to forget the sickening sensation of finding it. Yet that is the occupational hazard of a working strategist, a conscientious designer of what may be called "conflict-solving systems" — that is,

---

[7] *Ibid.*, p. 259. I have discussed this and related predictions by scientists in "Nuclear Sharing: NATO and the N + 1 Country," *Foreign Affairs*, Vol. 39, April 1961.

systems for keeping the peace or fighting a war, where the opponents' countermeasures must be taken into account. Thus the honest strategist must wear two or more hats, and this can be something of a personal strain. It can actually lead to quarrels among friends and organizations. The inventor of an ingenious measure may come to regard the inventor of an even more ingenious countermeasure with some distaste or even detestation. Whose side does the fellow think he is on?

All of which is true enough for the design of some national or alliance weapon system for possible use in a war. The personal strain and the strain on friendship is likely to be even worse where the system to be designed is an international control system. For while with national defense measures the element of at least partial opposition by an enemy is, or always should be, as plain as can be, it is not so plain in the case of an international system. Here one has an agreement with an adversary, and it is tempting to believe that he will cooperate. A scientist who works on evasion schemes is almost certain to be regarded as a leper. Isn't he opposing the agreement and ruining the possibility of international control? This is a nearly universal attitude. It was frequently voiced in protest against studies of possible ways to evade the test ban. Now it may be that some of the men who find it easiest to work on evasion schemes are those who oppose the agreement. None the less, anyone who is soberly in favor of an agreement with adequate safeguards should systematically and seriously wear both hats all the time. Two illustrations will suffice to show how, in the case of the test ban, each of the two principal factions has found it hard to deal with countermeasures, except where these support a point of view it is propounding anyway.

First, Edward Teller: Dr. Teller in my view has performed an important service in helping to develop a test ban with adequate controls, by thinking ingeniously about the possibilities of evading the various control systems that have been proposed. On the other hand, when it has come to supporting his views on the importance of testing, he has argued that we would lose more than the Russians would if we both stopped testing. As the defender, in contrast to the aggressor, we have a harder job. Therefore, he reasons, testing will enable us to develop the more sophisticated weapons we need for use in defense. However, in this argument he ignores the fact that the Russians will also be developing their weapons of aggression as counters to our defense, and there is no *a priori* reason for believing that they won't make more rapid strides in their "easier" job than we in our difficult one. In the past the development of nuclear weapons has favored the offense. In short, when it comes to the exploitation of tests in the development of weapons, Dr. Teller ignores countermeasures; they do not suit his argument. He has been extremely ingenious in considering enemy countermeasures to thwart control systems; these countermeasures do suit his argument.

Next, Hans Bethe: Dr. Bethe has been the symmetrical opposite of Dr. Teller on this matter as on others. As far as evasion schemes are concerned, he has said that he was embarrassed at presenting to the Russians the possibility conjured up by another American because it "implied that we considered the Russians capable of cheating on a massive scale. I think that they would have been quite justified if they had considered this an insult." [8] This suggests that it is all right to set up a police system, but not against potential crooks. His own energies in any case were devoted to the measures rather than the countermeasures. On the other hand, when it came to evaluating the military worth of weapons that might be developed with the aid of testing, such as anti-missile missiles, Dr. Bethe could frequently think of nothing except enemy countermeasures that would reduce their military worth nearly to zero. Dr. Bethe, like Blackett, is, without any extensive study, quite certain that enemy countermeasures like decoys would make a defense against ballistic missiles useless — or even harmful — in any reasonably likely contingency.

There are two points which emerge from this discussion of countermeasures. First, most physical scientists and engineers find it hard to deal with an enemy countermeasure, except where it spoils a system they themselves dislike on other grounds. This, I believe, is sometimes associated with an aversion to putting the fact of hostility in the center of their attention. Many of the articulate scientists, especially when considering arms-control agreements, prefer to think of harmony rather than conflict. The difficulty they have in contemplating countermeasures stems from hostility to the fact of hostility itself. In this way they slip more easily into the role of prophet and agent of a perfectly peaceful world.

The second point is that the evaluation of countermeasures in military conflict systems is likely to be very complicated, requiring

[8] "The Case for Ending Nuclear Tests," *The Atlantic Monthly*, August 1960, p. 46.

painstaking analysis, seldom undertaken by the technologists themselves. It involves for one thing an extensive canvass of potential
military operations on both sides and their possible interactions, and
sometimes a consideration of allies and more than one adversary; I
believe neither Dr. Teller nor Dr. Bethe has done this sort of systematic analysis of the military worth of the weapons they talk
about. Both are experts in the basic technology of bomb design, but
that is quite another matter.

Questions of military worth are broader than physics and in some
ways harder. They of course are not purely military questions any
more than they are purely technological. They may involve a forbid-
ding nest of problems including political and economic, as well as
military and technological, questions. However, on the questions
that have called for systematic analysis, characteristically there has
been no experience that was precisely relevant. For these questions
relate to a near or distant future affected by novel techniques and
political uncertainties. Experts are seldom "expert beyond experience," and analysis is needed, not to replace intuition, but to sharpen
and supplement it, and to make it more public and verifiable.

The role of uncertainty in decision-making as well as in system
studies to aid decision is so prominent that it is worth dwelling on,
especially as it is related in several ways to some recent obscuran-
tism. Attempts to prepare for anything other than the probable
events are branded as "paranoid" by Erich Fromm. By this definition, all of us who live in normally fire-safe neighborhoods and
houses and none the less take out fire insurance are paranoid. On
the contrary, it would be simply irrational to stake everything on a
"most likely" event where the uncertainties are so large and intrinsic.
This would be true even if we were quite sure we knew which were
the "most likely" events and could agree on what are useful objectives in these contingencies.

The scientists have been very far from agreement. In retrospect,
their views since World War II on major strategic issues — the
feasibility and usefulness, in deterring or fighting a war, of active or
civil defense, of the ability to bomb enemy industry or cities or military forces, of tactical nuclear weapons, of restraint in nuclear war,
and many others — show an extraordinary sequence of sudden and
repeated reversals.[9] The principal factions of scientists have re-

[9] An account of this history is given in my monograph, previously referred to,
which will be published in the fall.

mained in opposition — sometimes, however, almost exactly changing place. Moreover, the thought devoted to defining these issues and the evidence gathered for resolving them in no case warranted the certainty with which opposing views were propounded. This is not to say, of course, that "the politicians and the generals," with whom the physical scientists are contrasted, have been right. It would be hard to show, however, that the scientists have been on the whole more realistic or more prescient. Moral certainty and feelings of prescience have been a pretty uncertain guide to the future — even to the immediately next future beliefs of the prophets.

The gift of prescience is not only hard to come by for oneself; it is difficult to identify in others. Snow, who should be a great connoisseur of prescience, has run into difficulties. He derides Lindemann for backing infrared detection: "This seemed wildly impracticable then. . . . It seems even more wildly impracticable now."[10] Chinese Communist pilots downed by Sidewinder missiles with infrared homing devices would disagree. This would appear to be a case, in short, where Lindemann's prescience exceeds Snow's present knowledge of what has long since happened. Snow — and Blackett — take much too literally one of the lessons Snow draws from his cautionary tale: "The prime importance, in any crisis of action, of being positive what you want to do. . . . It is not so relevant whether you are right or wrong."[11]

In fact, serious study of the large uncertainties in the major strategic choices we have had to make suggests the opposite. Bertrand Russell in a better day once said, perhaps overstating the matter a bit: "The opinions that are held with passion are always those for which no good ground exists; indeed the passion is the measure of the holder's lack of rational conviction."[12] Passionate assurance on these intrinsically uncertain matters is not justifiable on logical grounds. Some technologists who are most articulate on matters of public policy in the defense and arms-control field should worry us most in their moments of boundless conviction, when they assume the role of seers. The tentative and fallible methods they have used professionally seem even more appropriate in the complex and uncertain areas of cardinal choice.

[10] *Science and Government, op. cit.,* p. 34.
[11] *Ibid.,* p. 73.
[12] Quoted by Charles Hussey in "Earl, Philosopher, Logician, Rebel," *The New York Times Magazine,* May 13, 1962, p. 10.

Don Price, in a brilliant article, "The Scientific Establishment," has developed with admirable lucidity the difference between the role of the scientist in the United States and the picture that Snow attributes to the United States, the United Kingdom and the Soviet Union.[13] In the United States the scientists have had unmatched opportunities for getting a direct political hearing for their ideas on policy. On every one of the cardinal choices cited by Snow, scientists have been heard, and by top decision-makers. On the other hand, I know of no clear evidence that in the Soviet Union scientists have affected the cardinal choices either on the basis of their prescience or on the basis of systematic study of major alternatives.

In the United States the problem of scientists and strategists is, I think, by and large not so much in being heard as in *saying* something, that is, saying something that is the result of thought and empirical study.

IV

It is high time that we recognized the extreme implausibility of the notion that war may become "impossible" in the next short space of time. On the other hand, neither is nuclear war inevitable in the next ten years, or many more. Since reducing the likelihood of war will preoccupy us for many years to come, it is appropriate to think of the probable consequences of this persisting preoccupation, some of which are already visible.

Decision-makers are likely to acquire a deep familiarity with these problems in the course of time, and to grow in professional competence in the continuing work on their solution. This is happening today, for example, in the Department of Defense. A year ago *The New York Times* published a statement of the Secretary on the issues in the choice of strategic bombardment vehicles for the late 1960's and after.[14] Whether or not we agree with the specific choice it explains, the document is an impressive one. In its thoughtful treatment of the uncertainties and the essential technological as well as operational and economic problems, it compares very favorably in sophistication with the analyses done by scientists to aid decision during World War II. Moreover, anyone who follows the Congressional Hearings will be quite convinced that such statements are comprehensively understood by a good many current decision-

---

[13] *Science*, June 29, 1962, pp. 1099–1106.
[14] *The New York Times*, March 16, 1962, pp. 1 and 12.

makers. These cardinal strategic decisions in general *are* made by them.

There is a good deal of hocus-pocus in Snow's pronouncement that the decision-makers "cannot have a first-hand knowledge of what those choices depend upon." [15] There is, of course, a sense in which nobody can have first-hand knowledge of *all* the things such decisions depend upon. They depend upon a great many things besides technology, in many fields. However, the choices that Snow dwells on, for example in his cautionary tales, are not all that obscure, and a first-rate Cabinet officer or military man can master the essentials of much more complicated matters, especially if they keep coming up. And they do.

The other side of this picture is that the natural and behavioral scientists, who offer advice or do analyses to assist decision, may experience a growth of professional competence too. Offhand judgments of individuals and crash studies by committees will always be with us and should. But expertise and committee activities have limitations. An expert on the whole range of problems involved in even one of these complicated choices is hard to find, and if one is discovered, the way in which he reaches his conclusion may be difficult to reproduce and verify; this in turn affects whether his judgment will be subject to criticism by more than a "handful of men." Inexplicitness is likely to be even worse with committees, since they proceed frequently by bargaining rather than reason. But explicit statement of the way conclusions are reached and of the evidence is part of the normal method of science, and what I mean by "conflict-systems studies" is simply the application of the method of science to the analysis of political-military strategic alternatives.

This suggests a little of the answer to at least one of the large questions with which we began: Both the physical and the behavioral sciences have a role to play in component research on cardinal choices. And in the course of studying strategic alternatives the methods of science can be used to reach conclusions going beyond the skills of any of the individuals involved. The important point is that on these complex cardinal questions, answers are won precariously and intermittently, in the course of hard empirical inquiry into the major factors affecting choice. Intuition and intelligence help, but do not make superfluous the study not only of the vital technologies, but also of the behavior of men and nations using, and

[15] *Science and Government, op. cit.*, p. 1.

affected by the use of, such technologies. No one has the gift of reliable foresight on these cardinal choices. The primary thing, then, is *not* to be positive. The basic failure of the physical scientists and engineers in their turbulent history during the cold war is not their lack of prescience but their acting frequently as if they had it.

CONTEXTS AND CONSTITUENTS

10   Congress

The authority of Congress in foreign policy appears to be increasing, as the boundaries of foreign and domestic policy become more and more obscure, and as the dollar cost of foreign policy programs requires Congressional authorization. The first of the two selections that follow, a legislative history of the foreign aid bill of 1961, conveys something of the scope and nature of the Senate's involvement in this one policy area.

But we may question whether the enlargement of foreign policy concerns in American political life actually means a dramatic increase in the power of Congress in foreign affairs, or in the significance of foreign affairs for the average congressman. The characteristics of contemporary foreign policy — its intricacies, its dangers and risks, its requirements for specialized skills and information, for secrecy — militate, as the first article pointed out, against an active role of any consequence for the Congress. In addition, there are many other tempting areas in which the congressman may work and make his mark. The second selection gives us some perspective on the congressman's perspective on foreign policy — on the way he evaluates this as a field of possible specialization for himself.

The Foreign Assistance Act of 1961

COMMITTEE ON FOREIGN RELATIONS, UNITED STATES SENATE

PRESIDENT'S PROPOSAL

On March 22, 1961, President Kennedy sent his first message on foreign aid to the Congress. Terming the years ahead as the "decade of development," the President called for —

1. Unified administration and operation — a single agency in Washington and the field, equipped with a flexible set of tools, in place of several competing and confusing aid units.

2. Country plans — a carefully thought through program tailored to meet the needs and the resource potential of each individual country, instead of a series of individual, unrelated projects. Frequently, in the past, our development goals and projects have not been undertaken as integral steps in a long-range economic development program.

3. Long-term planning and financing — the only way to make meaningful and economical commitments.

4. Special emphasis on development loans repayable in dollars — more conducive to businesslike relations and mutual respect than sustaining grants or loans repaid in local currencies, although some instances of the latter are unavoidable.

5. Special attention to those nations most willing and able to mobilize their own resources, make necessary social and economic reforms, engage in long-range planning and make the other efforts necessary if these are to reach the stage of self-sustaining growth.

6. Multilateral approach — a program and level of commitments designed to encourage and complement an increased effort by other industrialized nations.

7. A new agency with new personnel — drawing upon the most competent and dedicated career servants now in the field, and attracting the highest quality from every part of the Nation.

8. Separation from military assistance — our program of aid to social and economic development must be seen on its own merits, and judged in the light of its vital and distinctive contribution to our basic security needs.

Reprinted from the *Legislative History of the Committee on Foreign Relations*, United States Senate, 87th Congress, Washington, D.C., U.S. Government Printing Office, 1962, pp. 1–9.

He also stated that the $4 billion requested by the Eisenhower administration in the fiscal year 1962 budget would be allocated as follows: $1.6 billion for military assistance, $1.5 billion for grants, $900 million for long-term economic development loans financed through public debt transactions together with advance public debt authorizations of $1.6 billion for each of the succeeding 4 years for the same purpose.

On May 26, the President transmitted his detailed legislative recommendations in an executive communication accompanied by draft legislation which was introduced by Senator Fulbright the same day as S. 1983. The bill, as introduced, replaced the Mutual Security Act of 1954, as amended, and repealed that act except for minor provisions relating to various refugee and other programs.

Part I of S. 1983, entitled "The Act for International Development," encompassed the nonmilitary programs and included the President's recommendations for long-term development loans. The statement of policy was simplified. In addition to the $900 million for fiscal year 1962, and the $1.6 billion for each of the succeeding 4 fiscal years, to be financed by public debt transactions rather than appropriations, the authority to use dollar repayments of earlier loans, estimated at $1.5 billion over the 5-year period, was requested. Another change from then existing law was a provision requiring repayment of the development loans in dollars rather than permitting repayment in either dollars or local currencies.

Other provisions of part I authorized $380 million for development grants (a combination of the technical assistance and special assistance categories in previous laws); the issuance up to $1 billion of investment guarantees against loss from nonconvertibility, expropriation, war, revolution, insurrection, or civil strife, including authority to issue up to $100 million worth of "all-risk" investment insurance; the appropriation of $5 million for surveys of investment opportunities by private enterprise "other than in extractive industries"; $20 million for development research; $153.5 million for U.S. participation in various U.N. voluntary programs; $581 million for supporting assistance, formerly termed "defense support"; and $500 million for the contingency fund.

Part II of S. 1983, entitled "The Act of International Peace and Security," contained authorization for the appropriation of "such sums as may be necessary from time to time to carry out the purposes of this part" which provision would obviate annual authorizations of appropriations for military assistance. It was the intention of the administration to seek an appropriation of $1,885 million for fiscal year 1962. The President also asked for a continuation of his authority to sell arms already in stock for dollars. Finally, part II would authorize him to transfer up to $400 million worth of arms from Defense Department stocks to other nations, "subject to subsequent reimbursement" from "subsequent appropriations" for military assistance.

Other parts of S. 1983 authorized the President to exercise the functions set forth in the bill through any agency or officer of the United States and contained other administrative provisions. Although the establishment of a new agency was not spelled out in the bill, the President in his communication announced his intention of abolishing the Development Loan Fund and the International Cooperation Administration (ICA) and establishing an Agency for International Development (AID). Accordingly, S. 1983 included provisions for transfer of personnel and other authorities incident to the operations of the aid program.

Committee Action

Since S. 1983, as introduced, represented the first major redrafting of foreign aid legislation since 1954 and contained important new features as well as changes in emphasis, the bill became the subject of most intense and thorough committee consideration beginning May 31 with the appearance of Secretary Rusk. In 14 subsequent days in executive and public session the committee heard testimony from these principal administration witnesses: Secretary of the Treasury, Douglas Dillon; Secretary of Defense, Robert S. McNamara; the Chairman of the Joint Chiefs of Staff, Gen. Lyman Lemnitzer; the U.S. Representative to the United Nations, Adlai Stevenson; the Under Secretary of State for Economic Affairs, George Ball; and Assistant Secretary of Defense for International Security Affairs, Paul Nitze. Mr. Henry Labouisse, Director of both the International Cooperation Administration and the President's Foreign Aid Task Force, and Frank M. Coffin, Managing Director of the Development Loan Fund, testified, and were available to the committee throughout the course of the hearings. Other members of the President's Foreign Aid Task Force and representatives from the Department of State, ICA, and Defense also testified.

In addition to the executive branch witnesses, the committee had testimony from Senator Everett M. Dirksen, of Illinois, and from a number of public witnesses. These included representatives of the International Chamber of Commerce, the U.S. Chamber of Commerce, the National Council of Churches of Christ, the Citizens Foreign Aid Committee, the AFL-CIO, the American Farm Bureau Association, Americans for Democratic Action, the National Association of Home Builders, the League of Women Voters, the National Congress of Parents and Teachers, the Citizens Committee for UNICEF, the International Economic Policy Association, the Committee for a Democratic Spain, the Women's International League for Peace and Freedom, the Friends Committee on National Legislation, the Cooperative League of the U.S.A., the General Board of Christian Social Concerns of the Methodist Church, the Board of Missions of the Methodist Church, and the Council for Christian Social Action of the United Church of Christ. As in past years the nongovernmental testimony was predominantly favorable to the program.

On June 26 the committee began marking up the bill in executive session. During this meeting and subsequent meetings on June 28, July 6, 7, 10, 13, 14, 17, 18, 19, 20, and 21, the committee went over the bill section by section and also gave careful consideration to each amendment which had been proposed by any Member of the Senate. On July 24, the committee voted 13 to 4 to report the bill favorably as amended.

The committee approved main features of the President's program as it was submitted. The following table [on p. 162] shows the appropriations authorized in the bill as reported by the committee together with the amounts requested by the administration.

The following were the major changes made by the committee's amendments:

(1) In lieu of approving the use of dollar repayments of prior dollar loans, the committee added an equivalent amount ($287 million for fiscal year 1962 and $300 million each for fiscal years 1963–66) to the annual public debt transaction authority.

(2) The all-risk guaranty was limited to 75 per cent of the investment. The words "revolution, insurrection and civil strife" also were dropped from the enumeration of risks against which guaranties could be made.

(3) Instead of providing for the appropriation of $20 million for

	Administration Request	Committee Authorization
	(In millions)	
Development grants	$380.0	$380.0
Investment surveys	5.0	5.0
Development research	20.0	*
International organizations	153.5	153.5
Supporting assistance	581.0	450.0
Contingency fund	500.0	300.0
Military assistance	1,885.0	† 1,800.0
Administrative expenses	51.0	51.0
Total	3,575.5	3,139.5
Borrowing authority	900.0	1,187.0
Loan repayments	287.0	—
Total	1,187.0	1,187.0
Grand total	4,762.5	4,326.5

* Authority to spend funds available for pt. 1.

† The committee imposed a $55,000,000 ceiling on military assistance to be furnished to Latin America. A sum equal to the amount by which the ceiling reduced the military program planned for Latin America this year was to be transferred to the funds made available for development grants in that area.

development research, the committee authorized the use of that amount from other part I funds.

(4) As the table above shows, the committee cut $131 million from the President's request for supporting assistance and $200 million from the contingency fund.

(5) In lieu of the permanent authorization for military assistance appropriations, the committee authorized $1.8 billion each for fiscal years 1962 and 1963. The President's request for transfer authority of up to $400 million of arms from current stocks was reduced by the committee to $200 million.

FLOOR ACTION

Senate debate on S. 1983 began on August 4 and ended on August 18, 1961. Sixty-four amendments were offered. Most of these were discussed and voted on. Debate centered on the requested long-term borrowing authority and several amendments were directed toward that provision. The first of these to be voted on after considerable debate was Senator Byrd of Virginia's amendment, which would have replaced the long-term financing provisions of the bill by a requirement for annual appropriations rather than by public debt transactions. The Byrd amendment was rejected on August 11 by a vote of 39 to 56. Discussion next centered on an amendment by Senators Saltonstall, Keating, Bush, Dodd and Scott which would have required the submission of loan proposals over $10 million to the Congress and provided for a 30-day period within which such loans could be disapproved by concurrent resolution. This amendment did not come to a vote because the debate shifted to one offered by Senator Hickenlooper which in its original form required the transmission to Congress of a budget for the Development Loan Fund annually and the enactment of legislation approving the loan budget. Subsequently Senator Hickenlooper modified his amendment to provide also that congressional action on the annual Development Loan Fund budget take place in an appropriation bill. To the modified Hickenlooper amendment Senator Dirksen offered a substitute, which — after modification — required the President to submit loan plans of $5 million or more to the Senate Foreign Relations and the House Foreign Affairs Committees and the House and Senate Appropriations Committees 30 days prior to making a firm commitment and specified that any of these committees within that period could report a concurrent resolution, having highest floor priority, to disapprove such loan. The Dirksen substitute, as modified, was agreed to by a vote of 52 to 44, and the Hickenlooper amendment as amended by the Dirksen substitute by a vote of 63 to 34.

The Senate then turned to the other amendments. Agreed to were the following: Javits amendment providing that, wherever appropriate, programs of assistance were to be carried out through private channels and, to the extent practicable, in conjunction with local or governmental participation (voice vote); Lausche amendment providing that no guarantee of certain equity investments should assure against loss from normal business-type risks (voice vote); Magnuson amendment providing that U.S. dollars should be made available for marine insurance on certain commodities (voice vote); Fulbright substitute, by a vote of 48 to 45, for Williams amendment (barring loaning or reloaning from the Development Loan Fund at rates of interest in excess of 8 per cent) which would have provided that funds were not to be loaned or reloaned at rates considered excessive by the Development Loan Committee, but the amendment as amended was then withdrawn by Senator Williams; Bridges amendment barring voluntary contributions to any organization of which Red China is a member (voice vote); modified Bridges amendment making transactions of the Development Loan Fund subject to audit (voice vote); Ellender amendment reducing the loan fund authorizations for fiscal year 1963 through 1966 from $1.9 billion to $1.7 billion per year (51 to 43); another Ellender amendment reducing by $250 million the authorization for military assistance for fiscal year 1962 and fiscal year 1963 (57 to 37); Fulbright amendment to extend investment guarantee provisions to wholly owned foreign subsidiaries of American corporations (voice vote); Smathers amendment expressing the sense of the Congress in favor of pilot housing projects in Latin American countries (voice vote); McClellan amendment limiting the amount of domestic excess property that might be acquired or transferred (voice vote); modified Bush amendment to Dodd amendment to bar funds to any country unless the President has determined it was not dominated by international communism (61 to 34); the Dodd amendment itself, thus amended, by a vote of 93 to 0; Hickenlooper amendment providing that to the extent feasible, employees assigned to foreign duty should be assigned to countries and positions for which they had special competence (voice vote); Williams (Delaware) amendment providing that Treasury borrowing for financing of the Development Loan Fund should be at a rate of interest comparable to the current rate on U.S. obligations of a similar nature (voice vote); Randolph amendment providing that in the appointment of the 12 officers responsible for administration of the Development Loan Fund due consideration should be given to qualified professional engineers (voice vote); Humphrey amendment providing for utilization of appropriate Federal agencies in the operation of the technical assistance programs in the fields of housing, health, education, and agriculture (voice vote); Smathers amendment respecting resettlement of refugees from foreign countries (voice vote); Monroney amendment permitting the President to lend no more than 10 per cent of the funds made available for the Development Loan Fund to the International Development Association (voice vote); Morse amendment respecting expenditure of funds for internal security purposes in Latin America (voice vote); Gruening amendment providing that loans from the Development

Loan Fund might not be reloaned within the recipient country at rates of interest in excess of 5 per cent per annum more than the interest rate charged by the United States, by a vote of 74 to 16 after the rejection of a Sparkman substitute by a vote of 38 to 53; Sparkman amendment favoring the maximum use by aid recipients of low-cost fuels available in the free world (voice vote); Dirksen amendment barring aid to any country owing uncontested debts to a U.S. citizen who had exhausted available legal remedies (voice vote); Fulbright amendment providing authorization for Department of State administrative expenses for work under the bill (voice vote); and modified Humphrey amendment to encourage development and use in recipient countries of cooperatives, credit unions, and savings and loan associations (voice vote).

A number of amendments, on the other hand, were rejected by the Senate. They were: Ellender amendment to reduce authorization for military assistance by $500 million for each of the 2 fiscal years covered in the bill (38 to 57); Lausche amendment to reduce by $287 million in fiscal year 1962 and by $300 million for fiscal years 1963–66 the authorization of public debt transactions by the Development Loan Fund (46 to 46); Ellender amendment limiting U.S. contributions to U.N. programs in the Congo to 40 per cent of the total assessments (44 to 51); Capehart amendment providing that funds used for procurement outside of the United States of equipment or engineering services should be used for such procurement only within the country in which the project was located (27 to 67); modified Church amendment placing restriction on military grant aid to countries of Western Europe (22 to 70); modified Capehart amendment to limit to 3 years rather than 5 years the borrowing authority to finance the Development Loan Fund (45 to 50); another Capehart amendment providing that at least 50 per cent of all loans from the Development Loan Fund be made to private industry (33 to 63); Prouty amendment to require advance reports to Congress on all economic grants abroad exceeding $5 million (30 to 60); Cotton amendment to bar aid to countries exporting arms or strategic materials to Communist bloc countries (43 to 45); modified Miller amendment barring development loans and grants to any government more than 2 years in arrears in payment of its U.N. assessments, unless the President determined there was a reasonable assurance of such payments (24 to 66); and Dirksen amendment barring loans or grants for plants which would compete with U.S. industry (division).

Before the final vote on the bill, the Senate also agreed by a vote of 51 to 40 to a Mansfield motion to table an amendment by Senator Mundt and a number of others which would have extended the Federal aid to education program for impacted areas. With the committee amendments, which had been agreed to en bloc earlier in the debate, and the aforementioned additional amendments, the Senate passed S. 1983 on August 18 by a vote of 66 to 24.

HOUSE ACTION

Debate in the House, in the meantime, had begun and it came to a close also on August 18, when the House passed its companion bill, H.R. 8400, by a vote of 287 to 140. That bill, as reported by the House Committee on Foreign Affairs, was in all major respects similar to the Senate-passed bill. The few notable differences were the long-term borrowing authority which the House committee agreed to in the form submitted by the President; a cut of $100 million in supporting assistance as against the Senate committee's cut of $131 million; a cut in the authorization of administrative expenses of $2 million as against the Senate committee's approval of the whole amount; a provision in the statement of policy requiring foreign aid to be administered to "give effect" to the principles of freedom of navigation and freedom of persons to travel and pursue lawful activities without discrimination as to race or religion; and another provision in the statement of policy stating opposition to the admission of Red China to the United Nations and to the recognition of Red China. The latter statement had been subscribed to by the Senate also, but as a separate item of legislation, Senate Concurrent Resolution 34.

During the floor debate in the House, however, numerous amendments were agreed to, one of major consequence. As in the Senate, the House debate revolved largely around the authorization of long-term development loans to be financed by Treasury borrowing. The first amendment eliminated the long-term borrowing authority and replaced it with an authorization of $1.2 billion for fiscal year 1962 to be provided by the appropriation method. The amendment was proposed by Representative Saund and was agreed to by a standing vote of 197 to 185. The House also agreed to amendments changing the title of the bill to "An act for peace and mutual progress with justice and freedom for all"; strengthening language regarding qualifications for aid plans; opposing recognition of Outer Mongolia and its admission to the United Nations; and many others.

CONFERENCE ACTION

Because of the major differences in the financing of long-term development loans contained in the Senate and House texts and the many lesser differences, the conferees met for 8 days, one of the longest conferences over a foreign aid bill.

Much time was taken on the development loan financing provisions. The compromise agreed on here was to authorize the appropriation of $1.2 billion for fiscal year 1962 and $1.5 billion for fiscal years 1963–66 for development lending operations. In addition, the conference agreement authorized the President to make loan commitments on the basis of the authorizations in advance of actual appropriations when he deemed this necessary and important. In such cases, he was required to notify the appropriate committees of the Senate and the Speaker of the House. Moreover, the conference version provided that authorized but unappropriated funds could be appropriated in fiscal years subsequent to the one that they were authorized for.

Other differences were resolved as follows: The Senate title, "Foreign Assistance Act of 1961," was retained. The House provisions relating to Red China and Outer Mongolia were deleted, as was the Senate provision denying voluntary contributions to organizations of which Red China was a member. In lieu of either Senate or House language, the conferees rewrote the portion of the statement of policy dealing with freedom of navigation so as to provide that economic aid be administered to promote the principles of freedom of navigation and free travel without regard to race or religion and to promote adjudication of differences between two countries having friendly relations with the United States. The words "revolution and insurrection" in the investment guarantee provisions were retained from the House version. The ceiling on the so-called all-risk investment guarantee was set at $90 million as against $100 million in the Senate bill, of which $10 million could be used to guarantee investments in Latin American housing projects (the Senate bill had provided for $15 million and the House nothing). The House provisions prohibiting aid to Cuba and authorizing the President to establish a trade embargo were kept by the conferees but another one deny-

Fiscal Analysis of Foreign Assistance Program for Fiscal Year 1962

(In thousands of dollars)

Program	Authorization, Fiscal Year 1962				Appropriation, Fiscal Year 1962			
	Administration Request	Senate Bill	House Bill	Public Law 87-195	Administration Request (Revised)	House Bill	Senate Bill	Public Law 87-329
Pt. I. Act for International Development								
Ch. 2. Development Assistance:								
Title I – Development Loans	* $900.0	† $1,187.0	$1,200.0	‡ $1,200.0	$1,200.0	$1,025.0	$1,200.0	$1,112.5
Title II – Development Grants	380.0	380.0	380.0	380.0	380.0	259.0	§ 334.1	§ 296.6
Title III – Development Research	20.0	–	–	–	20.0	–	–	–
Title IV – Investment Surveys	5.0	¶ 5.0	¶ 5.0	¶ 5.0	5.0	¶ –	¶ 3.0	¶ 1.5
Ch. 3. International Organizations and Programs	153.5	153.5	153.5	153.5	153.5	153.5	153.5	153.5
Ch. 4. Supporting Assistance	581.0	450.0	481.0	465.0	581.0	400.0	450.0	425.0
Ch. 5. Contingency Fund	500.0	300.0	300.0	300.0	500.0	175.0	300.0	275.0
Pt. II. International Peace and Security Act								
Ch. 2. Military Assistance	**	†† 1,550.0	‡‡ 1,800.0	§§ 1,700.0	1,885.0	1,600.0	1,700.0	1,600.0
Pt. III								
Ch. 2. Administrative Expenses	51.0	51.0	49.0	50.0	51.0	45.0	50.0	47.5
Administrative Expenses (Department of State)	¶¶	¶¶	¶¶	¶¶	–	–	6.0	3.0
Total, all parts	2,590.5	4,076.5	4,368.5	4,253.5	4,775.5	3,657.5	4,196.6	3,914.6

[See explanatory footnotes on page 169.]

ing aid to nations which assisted Cuba was not. The Senate language denying assistance to Communist-dominated nations was agreed to rather than the House language which listed these nations. Two House provisions designed to assist farmers in recipient countries were modified and agreed to by the Senate. The Senate conferees also agreed to, in modified form, certain House provisions for an Inspector General, Foreign Assistance. In lieu of originally more restrictive House language, the conferees also agreed to prohibit loans for construction or operation of a productive enterprise directly in competition with U.S. enterprises unless the recipient nation agreed to limit exports to the United States to 20 per cent of the total annual production of this enterprise. The Senate amendment relating to interest rates, for which the House had no similar provision, was modified to require that "funds made available for this title shall not be loaned or reloaned at rates of interest excessive or unreasonable for the borrower and in no event higher than the applicable legal rate of interest of the country in which the loan is made."

There were a great number of other minor adjustments between the Senate and House which are explained in detail in the conference report (H. Rept. 1088). The conference report was adopted by a vote of 262–132 in the House and of 69–24 in the Senate on August 31.

The . . . table [on the facing page] shows the amounts authorized and appropriated for foreign aid for the fiscal year 1962.

---

* Borrowing authority. Additional borrowing authority of $1,500,000,000 for each of fiscal years 1963–66 was also requested together with the use of loan repayments estimated at $287,000,000 for fiscal year 1962 and $300,000,000 for each of fiscal years 1963–66.

† Borrowing authority. Additional borrowing authority of $1,500,000,000 for fiscal years 1963–66 contained in Senate bill. Use of loan repayments denied.

‡ Also authorized the appropriation of $1,500,000,000 for each of fiscal years 1963–66.

§ Included $100,000 special authorization for an American sponsored school in Poland.

¶ Authority to spend funds appropriated for pt. I substituted.

** Open-end authorization for fiscal year 1962 contained in Mutual Security Act of 1954, as amended.

†† Also authorized $1,550 million for fiscal year 1963.

‡‡ Also authorized an appropriation of such sums as may be necessary for fiscal year 1963.

§§ Also authorized an appropriation of $1,700,000,000 for fiscal year 1963.

¶¶ Open-end authorization contained in Mutual Security Act of 1954, as amended.

The Job of the Congressman

RAYMOND A. BAUER, ITHIEL DE SOLA POOL, AND LEWIS ANTHONY DEXTER

We have been converging on Congress by steps.[1] We began
with a consideration of the broadest group which might conceivably
be involved in the making of foreign-trade policy — the general
voting public. From there we moved to the American business
community — the broadest group which might be assumed to be
especially involved in the issue. Then we looked at a number of
communities — primary units in which interests may be organized
and expressed. Finally, our attention was turned to the organized
interest groups whose purpose was in whole or in part to influence
Congress in its decision on the Reciprocal Trade Act.

It should be noted that the very organization of this book implies
certain assumptions about the democratic process, assumptions
which in this section we wish to bring under explicit scrutiny.

In the classical literature on democracy, notably in the writings of
Burke, a lively debate concerned the question of whether the

Reprinted from Raymond A. Bauer, Ithiel de Sola Pool, and Lewis Anthony
Dexter, "The Job of the Congressman," *American Business and Public Policy:
The Politics of Foreign Trade* (New York: Atherton Press, 1963), pp. 403–13.
Reprinted by permission of the authors and the publisher, Atherton Press.

[1] This part of the book is based on "Congressmen and the People They
Listen To," by Lewis Anthony Dexter, submitted in partial fulfillment of the
requirements for the Ph.D. to Columbia University, 1959, here drastically con-
densed. The data arose mostly from interviews conducted by Dexter and the
other authors. Dexter's major assignment in 1954–1955 was to observe and to
interview on Capitol Hill. In all, about fifty members of Congress were interviewed, some several times. An equal number of closely affiliated persons, such
as administrative assistants, were interviewed, some on a continuing basis.
These interviews were supplemented by information from other sources. No
attempt was made to tabulate the interviews, since they followed the journalistic
principle of asking each man about those matters on which he had something
interesting to say, rather than the survey principle of asking each man the same
thing.

elected representative of the people should represent their interest as *he* sees it or as *they* see it. In either event, public opinion is regarded as pertinent, whether it be a constructive force guiding the representative's behavior or a corrupting force to which he makes concessions for the purpose of getting elected.

A neoclassical view of the democratic process, stemming from behavioristic political science, says in effect that it is naïve to think of legislators either as arriving independently at a decision in the general interest or as responding to the wishes of the general public. Organized special interests, according to this view, exercise the determining influence.[2] The general public, it asserts, lacks the capacity to make itself heard and, most especially, lacks the capacity to reward and punish legislators. The pressure groups which are articulate in presenting their views to Congress command attention because they, the pressure groups and not the general public, act to influence who will and will not be elected. In this view, organized pressure is the dynamo of politics.

One may well hold that all three models of the democratic process are correct in some instances and degrees. There are times when legislators out of their independent judgment arrive at decisions in the general interest. There are times when they respond to public opinion to the extent and in the sense they understand it, either because this corresponds to their ideal of democracy or because they wish to be re-elected. There are instances in which legislators succumb to the pressures of special-interest groups, as well as those in which they are under such pressures but resist them. A more sophisticated statement would hold that, in most legislative decisions, all three models apply to some extent. Often, the pressure of special-interest groups and of public opinion act as countervailing forces, offering the legislator independence in reaching a decision of his own choosing. Thus, what is involved is, not a single process, but a set of interacting processes.

This would, in any event, seem a sufficiently complicated way of looking at things, and it is approximately the model of the democratic process which was in our minds when we designed our study and gathered our data. Yet, even this eclectic model proved insuffi-

[2] Cf. [E. E.] Schattschneider [*Politics, Pressures, and the Tariff* (Englewood Cliffs, N.J.: Prentice-Hall, Inc., 1935)]; E. P. Herring, *Group Representation Before Congress* (Baltimore: Johns Hopkins Press, 1929); and D. Truman, *Governmental Process* (New York: Knopf and Company, 1951).

cient when it came to understanding just what went on in Congress. It was an inadequate representation of the forces and processes at work there.

The flaw in that model of the legislative decision-process was that it postulates certain issues and certain alternative solutions to them as given. It assumes that these issues are somehow there in the legislative arena and that the legislator finding the issues before him must pay attention to them and reach decisions on them. It pictures the legislator as much like a student before a multiple-choice examination, in which he faces fixed alternatives and selects an answer among them. The model with which we started and, for that matter, most decision theory concerns that kind of situation of defined options. The question asked by such theory is what groups or interests or forces operate to determine a choice, the alternatives being predefined.

What we actually found, on the contrary, was that the most important part of the legislative decision-process was the decision about which decisions to consider. A congressman must decide what to make of his job. The decisions most constantly on his mind are not how to vote, but what to do with his time, how to allocate his resources, and where to put his energy. There are far more issues before Congress than he can possibly cope with. There are very few of them which he does not have the freedom to disregard or redefine. Instead of choosing among answers to fixed issues, he is apt to be seeking out those issues that will meet fixed answers. He can select those issues which do not raise for him the Burkean dilemma; that is, he can select those issues on which he feels no special tension between his own views and those of his constituents.

The issues or answers the congressman chooses to deal with are largely determined by the kind of job he as an individual wishes to do. The model of the legislative decision-process toward which we inevitably moved was one dealing with the congressman's choices about his career, his professional identity, his activities, rather than one dealing primarily with choices about his policies. It was also a model which took as the relevant criterion for choice the over-all needs of his position, rather than the views on specific policies held by special groups of the public. Any model is a simplification which accounts for only a part of the observations. What we are asserting is that looking at how a congressman defined his job helped us account for his behavior on reciprocal trade as much as did looking at the foreign-trade issue or at the involvements in it of his constituents and other groups.

We were thus forced to look at the Congressional process from a different perspective. What compelled us to do so was our own specific relationship to the problem under scrutiny. Frequently, social-science studies of public events proceed historically. The scholar begins with an event and seeks out antecedents that constitute a seemingly adequate explanation for the occurrence that is the focus of his interest. The actual nature of the consequent event serves him as a criterion of the relevance of prior events. He can ignore aspects which he might have thought relevant but for the wisdom of hindsight.

Our study was a historical one in the sense that we were interested in a single occurrence and its antecedent circumstances. But, since we were studying the event in the making, we could not use hindsight to know what would prove relevant to an event the ultimate shape of which we could not yet know. In the latter respect, our investigation was similar to an analytical-predictive one. In a strictly analytic study dealing with the interrelationship of a limited number of variables, the scholar's theoretical interests serve as a criterion of relevance. He is free to ignore factors which fall outside his theoretical scheme so long as this scheme yields a satisfactory pay-off. In an analytical-predictive study, statistical predictions are made on the basis of a limited analytic model. If a sufficient proportion of events in a given category are predicted correctly, one is satisfied.

Our study was also different from these in that we were trying to anticipate ("predict" would be too pretentious a word) what was going to be significant in a single instance, and we could not remain content with the general validity of our model. Thus, we could not study the single event, the controversy over the Reciprocal Trade Act, by itself. We had to look at it in the context of the other things which were going on in Congress at the same time. As we shall illustrate at length, this is not a simple statement of the truism that "everything is related to everything else."

Our frame of attention had to include more of what was going on in Congress while the Reciprocal Trade Act was being considered than it would if we had had knowledge of subsequent events to guide us. This section of the book is a systematization of certain features of the Congressional process that came to our attention while we were thus trying to anticipate and understand the events as they were taking place. It is an essay on some aspects of the Congressional process and not a history of the passage of the Reciprocal Trade Act in 1954 and 1955.

Choosing a Job

It is a cliché that the main job of a congressman is to be re-elected. There is much truth to it, but there are various ways of getting re-elected. Somehow, the congressman must do things which will secure for him the esteem and/or support of significant elements of his constituency. This he can achieve in many ways. He can seek for himself a reputation as a national leader, which may sometimes impress his constituents. He can work at press relations, creating and stimulating news stories and an image of activity. He can be a local civic leader, attending and speaking at community functions. He can make a reputation for himself in the field of legislation. In some states, he can be a party wheel horse and rely on the organization to back him. He can get people jobs and do social work and favors. He can become a promoter of certain local industries. He can conduct investigations and set himself up as a defender of public morals. He can take well-publicized trips to international hot spots. He can befriend moneyed interests to assure himself a well-financed campaign. He can befriend labor unions, veterans' organizations, or other groups with a numerous clientele and many votes. The one thing he cannot do is much of all these things. He must choose among them; he has to be a certain kind of congressman.

The reason he must choose is the scarcity of resources. Resources are various; they include time, money, energy, staff, information, and good will. All these have one common characteristic — there is never enough. They must all be budgeted and used with discretion. Opportunity is striking constantly or at least standing outside the door, but it is only occasionally that one has the wherewithal to capitalize on it. The skill of a congressman is to make the choices which, with the resources at hand, will get him the greatest results in doing the kind of Congressional job he has chosen to do.

Furthermore, his choices are not discrete. Choices on the use of scarce resources are never independent, for what is used for one purpose cannot be used for another. The choices are linked in other ways, too, for Congress is both a social system and part of a larger social system. The individuals with whom a legislator interacts in one transaction may be the same ones involved in another. The choice to spend time and effort in winning a particular friend can hardly be independent of another choice which would make of that person an enemy.

For these reasons, a rational congressman who has decided what kind of congressman he wants to be would then use his resources according to strategies consisting of whole packages of related acts. His stand on a particular issue would be far less dependent on what was specifically involved in that issue than on its role in a general policy or strategy on which he was working. Congressmen are no more rational political men than the businessmen whom we previously examined are rational economic men. Yet, to the extent that they are partially that and that a "maximizing" [3] model helps us understand their behavior, the model must be one relating continuing strategies, all aimed at achieving a certain kind of job success, not one dealing with strategies to maximize success on discrete issues. The skillful congressman — and, in this respect, most congressmen are skillful — makes his choices in terms of ways of living in a continuing political system. He constantly weighs his future relations with his colleagues.

A skillful congressman also takes account of the strategies of the other players in the Capitol arena and the rules of the game there. He is part of a multiperson game in which the goals of the different players vary and in which each defines them for himself; in which the pieces are the scarce resources which can be allocated; and in which the optimal strategies depend on the coalitions which can be formed, the procedural rules of the house in which the game is being played, and the power and the goals of the other players. Voting strategies depend on many things besides the pros and cons of issues. A senior senator, for example, can seek for himself the mantle of statesman with some chance of success, thanks to unlimited debate and his ability to balance special interests in one part of the state against those in another. A representative has far less chance of playing that particular kind of game. Again, a congressman can afford to vote the popular position in his constituency although he believes it wrong when he knows that there will be enough Congressional votes to defeat him anyway. He may have to vote his principles with courage when he thinks his vote is going to count.

[3] Actually, as already indicated, we believe Herbert Simon's concept of "satisficing" is more appropriate, though less familiar. [Cf. his *Models of Man* (New York: John Wiley, 1957), p. 261.]

But, even then, he may, if skilled at parliamentary procedure, satisfy his constituents by dramatic votes and gestures at moments when they cannot succeed.

How a congressman defines his job, the importance of choice in the use of his time and resources, the continuing character of Congress as a social system, and the constraints of procedure and interaction form the substance of this section. The congressman is typically thrust unprepared into a specialized milieu and confronted with a massive volume of highly technical legislation, with most of which he can deal only superficially. Counting on the assistance of a modest staff, he must work within the framework of a committee structure and is burdened with the additional task of servicing myriad personal requests from his constituents. These pressures combine to make time one of the congressman's most critical resources and the study of its allocation and husbanding a key to the legislative process.

ALLOCATING TIME

The scholar tends to approach his problem as though it had equal salience in the minds of men dealing with it on a practical basis. But we have already observed, in our study of the business community, that foreign-trade policy was only one of many issues crying for the American businessman's attention and not one of the most pressing. What has been said of the businessman must be said doubly of the congressman. There are infinite demands on him, which he must meet with finite means. Both the scholar and the newsman often miss this point in their assumption that congressmen can pay attention to all issues of national policy. We began our study with two major interests: legislation and communication. We wanted to know what congressmen did about tariff legislation, and we wanted to know what and who influenced them in what they did. We tended to assume that the issues of public policy which were crucial to us were as crucial to the men with whom we were talking. Yet, few congressmen viewed tariff legislation as their primary concern, and the way in which many of them noticed what they read and heard about reciprocal trade was in large part a consequence of the fact that tariff legislation was simply one of several competing interests for them.

The low priority assigned tariff matters and the effect of that on what congressmen heard and did may be examined by considering their allocation of time. We could equally proceed by looking at the allocation of any other resource, particularly good will, for that is one of the most essential commodities in which a politician deals — there are limits to the frequency with which he can draw on his available fund of it. But let us look here at the consequences of the shortage of time in the congressman's life. A congressman is a member of what sociologists call a free profession, in that he makes his working schedule for himself. His job is undefined and free, not only in schedule, but also in content and in standards of achievement. As a result, he lives under a heavy burden of multiple choices, and, what is more, the choices he has to make are far more fateful than those most citizens make. The citizen may conceive of the congressman tackling his highly responsible choices with the same care and awe with which the citizen imagines himself tackling the few really responsible choices which he makes. But, by the very nature of their busy lives, congressmen cannot do this.

Let us consider the ways in which a congressman may occupy his time. He may concentrate on any of the following aspects of his job:

1. Legislative planning — the working out of legislation in committee.
2. Legislative criticism — an unpopular role in the House, but one common in the Senate.
3. Parliamentary procedure — specializing in rules and regulations for the conduct of Congressional business.
4. Legislative tactics — like Lyndon Johnson when he was majority leader, or James Byrnes in an even earlier period.
5. Investigation.
6. Public education — rallying support for causes through forums, speeches, articles.
7. Personal advertisement and campaigning — birthday and condolence letters to constituents, congratulations to graduating high school seniors, news letters, press releases, trips back home.
8. Seeing visitors and shaking hands.
9. Personal service — rectification of bureaucratic injustices; facilitating immigration of relatives of constituents; arranging military leaves, transfers, and hardship releases; helping confused constituents to route their inquiries to the right administrative offices; providing information on social security rights, etc.
10. Representation of local or state interests — Sen. Wiley (R., Wis.), ranking Republican on the Foreign Relations Committee, reported: "In 1939 on the occasion of the 75th anniversary of the Wisconsin cheese industry, it was my pleasure to preside over an appropriate celebration in Washington. It featured the world's largest cheese. . . . The cheese

was eventually cut up and distributed . . . to Senators, Representatives, Congressional employees, newspapermen and others. . . . I am satisfied that advancing the interests of one of the foremost food industries of my state . . . is one of the jobs for which I was sent to Washington. . . ."[4]

11. Participating in national political organization or campaigning—for example, Sen. A. S. Mike Monroney (D., Okla.) has been chairman of the Speakers Division of the Democratic National Committee.

12. Development of local political organization and leadership — many senators are state political bosses, for example, the late Sen. Pat McCarran in Nevada.

A congressman might decide that his chief responsibility is, after all, legislation. Even so, there is far too much legislation for any particular legislator to attend to all of it. During the Eighty-third Congress, 1953–1955, which we were studying, the following legislative issues were among those considered:

1. Reciprocal Trade Extension acts of 1953 and 1954
2. Customs simplifications bills
3. Cargo Preference Act of 1954
4. Excise tax
5. Complete overhauling of federal tax system
6. Social security revision
7. Unemployment compensation measures
8. Appropriations measures
9. Amendment to the Constitution[5]
10. Civil service pay raises
11. The lease-purchase bill
12. Revision of health-welfare-grant formulas
13. Flexible price supports
14. Reduction of wheat acreage
15. Reduction of the Air Force
16. Establishment of an Air Academy
17. Building of twenty merchant ships
18. Upper Colorado development
19. Niagara Falls development
20. Highway aid
21. Commercial use of atomic-energy patents
22. Range improvements by private interests on public lands
23. Alaskan statehood
24. Hawaiian statehood

[4] A. Wiley, *Laughing with Congress* (New York: Crown Publishers, 1947), pp. 136–141. This book probably has the best treatment of the Congressional work load. It is one of the indispensable books about Congress for anybody trying to find out what Congress does. Especially valuable is Chapter VI, "The Office Inferno," particularly pp. 90–96.

[5] A resolution providing for the replacement of House members killed in a national emergency.

25. End of price controls
26. Revision of the Taft-Hartley Act
27. New health insurance law
28. Windfall profits
29. The Bricker amendment
30. Wiretap bills
31. Suffrage for eighteen-year-olds
32. Raising the federal debt ceiling
33. Tidelands oil
34. Sale of government rubber plants
35. Abolition of the Reconstruction Finance Corporation
36. The St. Lawrence Seaway
37. Special Refugee Immigration Law
38. Interest rate rise for Federal Housing Administration
39. Excess profits tax
40. Bill for twenty-six new judgeships
41. Witness immunity measures
42. Ten plans for government reorganization
43. Rise in postal rates.

In addition, during the Eighty-third Congress members of the Senate were confronted with a number of other time-consuming issues which were not properly legislative but were more important than many laws in terms of policy. Prominent among these were the censuring of Sen. Joseph McCarthy (R., Wis.), the proposal to unseat Sen. Dennis Chavez (D., N.M.), and the confirmation of appointments to major commissions, cabinet and diplomatic posts, and judgeships. Some appointments were highly controversial. The appointment and confirmation of ex-Representative Joseph Talbot (R., Conn.) to the Tariff Commission seems to have been regarded in many quarters as as great a protectionist victory as passage of the Fuel Oil Quota (Simpson) Bill would have been.

In the same session, the Senate and House conducted at least sixty-five investigations, some of which had specific legislative purposes. Finally, it should be considered that interested members of the House and Senate may and do devote long hours of work to legislative proposals that never reach the floor or achieve serious consideration in committee.

Only painstaking and continuous study can give a legislator command of the often complex details of any one of the many proposed pieces of legislation. Few congressmen can or do master more than a handful of them. A congressman with years of service may in time develop expertness in a particular field of legislation, but the best-informed of our lawmakers are fully acquainted with only a fraction of the bills that come before each session.

Furthermore, even if some particular legislation is the major focus of interest of a given congressman, usually, if he is to be re-elected, he cannot completely ignore other aspects of his job.[6] Said one administrative assistant:

> You know this business; it is like trying to deal with a great immovable beast or cleanse the Augean stables . . . you just cannot do much. . . . The Senator is now a member of fourteen important subcommittees, and he just cannot split up his time. . . . Now there is the [particular] subcommittee — . . . and all those questions are tremendous and vital questions. . . . Yet, you try to get these senators [members of the subcommittee] even to agree to meet at any one time and you cannot even do that . . . they are so independent and rushed and all doing things their own way.[7]

Not only is the congressman himself overcommitted, but he is surrounded by similarly busy men. A salient fact about the congressman's job is that what he does is invariably accomplished through other people, most of whom are as busy as himself. He becomes involved in a complex web of interdependence with colleagues and constituents as a result of the fact that each must work through the other to get what he wants, whether it be re-election, the passage of a piece of legislation, or service from a congressman. To anticipate a point which we shall develop later, it is highly naïve to think of

[6] For a variety of reasons, House members, if they are so minded, are freer to "take it easy" than members of the upper body. They represent a smaller constituency. Crucial decisions in the House are usually made by the leadership. Also, each member of the larger House is on fewer committees.

[7] A senatorial assistant rejected the idea of having an intern from the American Political Science Association in his office because "the intern has lots of ideas — mostly good — but every single one of them means more work." We should note that among the duties of a congressman is running his own office and staff. By 1959, House members received approximately $40,000 a year for the maintenance of staffs. They were permitted to employ as many as eight persons. In addition, members were allowed $1,200 per session for stationery, 2,700 minutes of telephone service, 12,000 words of telegraph service, $600 a year for official office expenses in the district, and $200 a year for air-mail and special-delivery stamps. Very few members employ as many as eight persons or spend quite the maximum. Few congressmen receive office space adequate for that number, and the use of a staff that large is likely to involve the personal financing of some office expenses.

The amount available to senators for staff purposes varies from state to state. The average expense appeared to be more than $50,000 a year. This usually permits the senator to employ two or three professional persons as legislative and administrative assistants and two or three clerks.

a congressman as being under pressure from one direction or even as being under cross-pressure from two opposing directions. More typically, he is under simultaneous influence and demands from many directions, a large number of which are relevant to the issue with which the scholar or interest group is concerned only in that they compete with that issue for the congressman's time and energies.

However, our purpose is not to argue that congressmen are busy people but to show specifically that their busyness affected their reaction to the reciprocal-trade extension.

Busyness blocked effective communication of constituents' views to their congressmen. A congressman can seldom readily inform himself as to how his constituents feel about any issue. A sense of acting in the dark about public opinion plagued many of the legislators we interviewed. On the simplest level, communications with respect to foreign-trade policy had to compete with, and frequently were lost in, the welter of other communications. This is particularly true of conversations which congressmen and their assistants had with other people. In 1955, a senator's assistant commented:

> You know, so many people have come into the office in the last two weeks on all these things — rubber disposal, stock market, reciprocal-trade extensions, and taxes — I just haven't been able to keep in mind which was which; and I think it is pretty difficult for the Senator to keep track, too.

One representative who was very much concerned with the Reciprocal Trade Act complained about his impossible work load. He had recently been back to his district; he could remember vaguely that a number of people had talked to him about tariff and foreign-trade policy, but he could not recall who had wanted what.

Both these men belonged to the committees which handled reciprocal-trade extension. Yet, even for them, it was but one issue among many. They had no time to give more than a hurried glance to communications about it. As a result, they, too, had only the haziest notion of what public opinion in their constituency really was. The communications they received were poorly remembered and ill-understood. Most messages left only the impression that something had been said, not a clear recollection of what was said. We find that the net effect of communication was to heighten attention to an issue, rather than to convey specific content about it.

11   Interest Groups

One of the myths about American politics and foreign policy that keeps reappearing concerns the supposedly strong and nefarious influences of private interest groups or "pressure groups." One of the remarkable features about this particular myth is that it manages to flourish even though there is very little evidence to support it. In the field of foreign economic policy, in particular, it is widely assumed that private economic groups are successfully bringing pressure to bear on their representatives in Congress to protect or advance their interests. The following selection, from a larger study of the politics of foreign trade in the 1950's, compels us to revise this assumption. The authors ask, what do interest-group activities and other political communications look like from the point of view of their targets, the congressmen?

Communications — Pressure, Influence, or Education?

RAYMOND A. BAUER, ITHIEL DE SOLA POOL, AND LEWIS ANTHONY DEXTER

We started with the notion that public officials would see themselves as under almost constant pressure from those who have a stake in the decisions they make. That seems to be the conven-

Reprinted from Raymond A. Bauer, Ithiel de Sola Pool, and Lewis Anthony Dexter, "Communications — Pressure, Influence, or Education?", *American Business and Public Policy: The Politics of Foreign Trade* (New York: Atherton Press, 1963), pp. 433–43. Reprinted by permission of the authors and the publisher, Atherton Press.

tional belief about pressure politics put forth in textbooks and journalistic accounts. It may in fact be an accurate description of what happens in some cases, such as post-office pay raises, patronage matters, in getting contracts for highway jobs, and similar issues on which the interests of the parties are clear, immediate, unequivocal, vital, and relatively uncomplicated by other relationships with the congressman which must be considered under the heading of long-run good will. But, for most general legislation, the picture is much like what we found in the foreign-trade area.

The first lesson we learned is that vigorous pushing of an interest is not necessarily regarded as pressure. One of our early talks was with an administrative official who had prepared a report minimizing the defense aspect of foreign economic policy. During the committee hearing, he had said with some exasperation to a questioner, "I suppose next you will tell me the toothbrush-makers need protection for national defense reasons." (We have changed the product.) Angry letters instigated by a lobbyist came to him from all over the country protesting his offense against that minor industry. But when our interviewer asked him, "Did other people put pressure on you in a similar way?" the official "looked . . . incredulous and said, 'Why he [the lobbyist] didn't put any pressure on me.'" Our interviewer insisted, but the respondent said vehemently: "No, I didn't have any pressure on me at all; if you are reasonable with these people, they are reasonable with you."

"Reasonable," "legitimate," and "threat" turned out to be key words.

We continued for a while to use the word "pressure" in our interviews, but steadily ran into the response: "What do you mean, 'pressure'? I wasn't under any pressure. It was all perfectly legitimate."

Or, as Congressman Second from New Anglia told us: although "the tariff was number two or perhaps number one" in what he heard from his district, "nobody's tried to pressure me. Yes, there have been a lot of letters about the damage they are suffering, but there has been no pressure — by that I mean no threats."

Vigorous representation of a partisan interest turns out to be per se legitimate, providing it is "reasonable," that is, devoid of threat.[1] Said one assistant, speaking of organized labor, "It's true the senator

[1] Cf. our fuller report on this point: Frank Bonilla, "When is Petition 'Pressure'?" *Public Opinion Quarterly*, Vol. XX, No. 1, Spring 1956, pp. 39–48.

opposed repeal of Taft-Hartley publicly, and they criticized him for it. But that was all in the game. Some of them may have thought he was sore about the way they took after him, but he expected it. He wasn't sore."

Most congressmen, and we believe to a lesser extent personnel in administrative agencies, believe strongly in the right of petition. Furthermore, they often regard the communications which come into their offices as helpful and instructive. True, persistent pleading of a cause to which the congressman is firmly opposed may eventually have an abrasive effect on his nerves. But, to our surprise, we found many congressmen looking to mail and personal contacts as sources of information on vital issues. This was more true of representatives than of senators, who are blessed with more adequate staffs.

We think it fair to say that, on general legislative problems, communications from constituents are seldom pressure — in the congressman's eye. The congressman perceives in them little or no element of external threat, which is what distinguishes petition from pressure. We have already seen that the constituents from whom the congressman hears are generally friendly and hesitate to alienate him on any single issue. Recall the farm delegation which approached a group of Southern congressmen and said: "The national told us to pass the word along; we're in favor of reciprocal trade, but we shan't get mad if you vote against it." We repeatedly ran across the theme: "So-and-so has gone along with us on so many issues that we wouldn't think of opposing him because he disagrees with us on this."

The word "pressure" does exist in Congressional parlance. It is used, for example, to explain the opposition's behavior, sometimes described as "opportunistic yielding to pressure." "Opportunism" and "pressure" are handy terms to explain why someone disagrees with you.

There is also reference to pressure on oneself. Sometimes the term "pressure mail" was applied to mail on the Reciprocal Trade Act. But "pressure" (if on oneself) most frequently referred to influence exerted by other congressmen or by the administration. An example of such pressure was Rayburn's injunction to freshman congressmen on the morning of the key foreign-trade votes that to "get along" they had better "go along." What made it pressure was the implied threat of disapproval by the powerful party leadership on which fate in Congress depends.[2] Similarly, the administration can apply pressure by threats to withhold patronage. Individual congressmen can also apply pressure by implying that they will not cooperate on other issues with the person being pressured. One congressman said that Rep. Cleveland Bailey (D., W. Va.) was "real rough" in attempting to get him to go along on a protectionist measure.

But does not the expression of a constituent's view and/or interest incorporate an implied threat to vote against a congressman who disagrees with him? It may. There have unquestionably been individual instances of congressmen being defeated because of their unpopular stand on a single issue. However, what is important is the fact that congressmen, though they definitely respond to mail and other communications, do not usually perceive in them any cause for alarm. One senator, out of curiosity, had his staff check on the writers of 100 letters he received advocating support of a higher minimum wage. It was found that seventy-five writers were eligible to register, but, of these, only thirty-three actually were registered. Furthermore, the letters advocated his support of a measure on which he had been particularly active, and the content of the mail showed no realization of the stand he had so publicly taken. The senator could scarcely get excited about these letter-writers, as sources of either opposition or support, on the basis of that issue. He might, however, respond to their petition as a legitimate request and an opportunity to make some voters among them familiar with him as a person.

Approximately the same result might generally be expected from an analysis of the mail. The reader will remember that most of the businessmen in our sample who had communicated with Congress were not aware of the position taken by the man to whom they had written. The probability is that they also did not follow up to see how he voted. Congressman Simpson received a number of letters and postcards in 1953 urging him to vote against the Simpson bill! We found that even some of the people active in the major interest groups were not aware of how key members of Congress had voted on the Reciprocal Trade Act.

In view of such circumstances, it is little wonder that congressmen do not regard partisan communications to them as a source of pres-

---

[2] We do not consider this a contradiction of our earlier statement that, in Congress, party discipline is much less important a factor than in most legislatures.

sure in the sense of an implied threat. However, to say that incoming communications are not perceived as pressure is by no means to say that congressmen are not responsive to them, particularly to mail from constituents.

Indeed, the mail is the congressman's main source of information on foreign-trade policy. Whenever we asked a congressman if he had heard anything about foreign-trade policy, he almost inevitably answered in terms of mail. We cannot say whether this is true of other issues, but it is our distinct impression that congressmen are far more conscious of what the mail says about foreign-trade legislation than they are about any other exposition of foreign-trade matters.[3]

Visitors and telephone-callers have an impact similar in character to that of mail. They are listened to as indicators of feeling back home. They too, however, seldom use pressure, nor do the professional lobbyists.

You know all these guys who come in here never talk about issues at all. I've seen lots of them supposedly lobbying. . . . We go out to lunch, but they don't necessarily talk about anything. [We] just know a good guy may be going out of business because he doesn't get more trade or so. It's the spirit that influences.

"The spirit" may be imperfect as a communication medium, but small talk does serve the congressman as a protection against having to reply with a face-to-face "No." Furthermore, congressmen frequently ask questions of visitors in ways which channel their comments in the direction desired. One congressman asked a delegation whether any of them really favored reciprocal trade. They did, but, on receiving this cue, they talked about other things. The typical business visitor to a Congressional office comes with not one problem, but several, and in general congressmen are much more experienced and expert at diverting visitors than visitors are in forcing congressmen on a point.

One source of word-of-mouth information is fellow-congressmen and other members of the Capitol Hill work force. The structure of Congress is such that every member has to specialize. As we have noted, the congressman cannot do all the things his job calls for. He can operate effectively only on that special part of the legislation which comes before the committees on which he sits. A given repre-

---

[3] This is, of course, not true of members of the relevant committees, who spend a great deal of time in hearings.

sentative or senator sits on one or two committees, and one will be of particular importance to him. Over a period of years, a capable congressman becomes an expert on the subject matter of his committee assignments. One man becomes a specialist on immigration and another on conservation, one on foreign policy and another on taxes. Among the specialists on any topic, there will be men of different character and viewpoint. Thus, congressmen develop an implicit roster of fellow-congressmen whose judgment they respect, whose viewpoint they normally share, and to whom they can turn for guidance on particular topics of the colleague's competence. Each congressman tends to follow the lead, not of any one person, but of a roster of specific colleagues sorted by topics.

Members of the House on the whole associate with other congressmen and assistants whose views are like their own. Much of the social life of Congress is passed with other members of the same party and their wives. It is especially from among these friendly associates that a congressman picks out as a mentor on a particular topic a man who is on the appropriate committee and who is a specialist on that topic. Communication with such a person may often be no more than an exchange of two sentences: "How should I vote on such-and-such bill?" and an answer.[4] Or it may be a validation of the authenticity of a partisan claim, for example, "Are oil imports really hurting your people?" Occasionally it will be fuller conversation, but even in the usual brief form it may be very effective.

Another source of Congressional information is the published word. With regard to reciprocal trade, except for newspapers, this played very little part in the legislative information system. With few exceptions, there was among our Congressional interviewees little indication of familiarity with the economic literature on international trade. On the other hand, perhaps a dozen congressmen referred to some item in the press, and several had evidently obtained ideas from newspaper columns. No respondent mentioned specialized, for example, business, newspapers. A few did refer to recently issued reports prepared by government agencies or interest groups, but these had been skimmed, rather than read. Congressmen seemed to have read somewhat less than had executive department

---

[4] A member of a state legislature told us that she could walk onto the floor during a roll call and count even on members of the opposition to tell her reliably what would be the "right" vote *for her,* considering her allegiances and interests.

officials whom we interviewed. It must, however, be remembered that there is little available in print which copes with the problem the congressman faces on tariff policy. What he essentially needs is material which reconciles the claims and desires of his individual constituents with over-all national economic problems. What he finds in print are for the most part theoretical and high-level discussions of national interest and economic policy, on the one hand, and discussions of the plight of some one industry, on the other, not material balancing the two.

We might also mention that we can recall nothing to indicate that nation-wide opinion-poll data had any appreciable impact on Congress. Members of the administration were anxious that our survey of business should be published [5] so that they could use the results. (We do not know whether they were ever used.) Some representatives did informal public-opinion polls in their own districts. But, on the whole, in the reciprocal-trade controversy, members of Congress paid little attention to general public opinion as it could have been ascertained by formal polling techniques.

Despite the fact that, on issue after issue, the mail has been shown to be not representative — in 1954–1955 it was about ten-to-one protectionist — and despite the fact that there is no reason to suspect that letter-writing on any given issue has any relationship to voting or political influence, the mail is nevertheless seen as the voice of the district or state. As is to be expected, many congressmen and senators run counter to the mail in obedience to dictates of conscience, party, or committee; but, when they do so, many of them appear to think that they are defying something very significant.

Why is the mail taken so seriously? First of all, members of Congress and their staff have no alternative but to spend an enormous amount of time reading and answering mail, and a busy man would be less than human if he were to believe he was wasting so much time. Second, congressmen often operate in a near-vacuum, uninformed about what their ultimate employers, the voters in their district or state, really want. The mail gives a sense, perhaps a spurious one, of receiving instructions on some issues. Such instructions give the man a sense of being in contact with his constituents and some notion, again perhaps spurious, as to what is likely to please his constituents and result in his re-election. Third, many junior members

[5] This was done in Raymond A. Bauer, Suzanne Keller, and Ithiel de Sola Pool, "The Shift in Business Opinion on the Tariff," *Fortune,* April 1955.

of the House, having no important role on major committees, appear to be frustrated at their inability to take any demonstrably effective action on major issues. Answering constituents' mail is one thing they can do which gives them the feeling of acting effectively. Fourth, writing to one's congressman is an expression of the citizen's right of petition — treasured by most congressmen — from perceived inequities of legislation or administrative action. Finally, some congressmen, whether realistically or not, appear to regard their correspondence as rational academic discussion of issues of national importance. Much Congressional correspondence serves no visible political or legislative purpose.

But mail must be "genuine." It must not be junk — that is, press releases or other broadcast mailings — nor must it be stimulated. Stimulated mail is not entirely easy to define. In its pure form, it consists of virtually identical postcard messages written at the instigation of a single company, union, or interest group. (One company even mailed the postcards for its workers, fearing that they would not know who their congressman was.) Congressmen look for signs of stimulation — similarity of phrasing ("They all used the same argument") or even stationery ("They handed out the paper") and time of mailing ("You could tell the hour or minute someone pushed the button"). Indeed, it is hard to fool a congressman as to when mail is stimulated. Some organizations urge their members to write in their own words, on their own stationery, and as personally as possible. Congressional assistants tell us that perhaps one in fifty persons who write such a letter will enclose the original printed notice from the organization urging an individualized, apparently spontaneous letter. But some mail which would have to be regarded as stimulated in the literal sense does not necessarily have the impact of stimulated mail. Pittsburgh Plate Glass, for example, succeeded in getting people in the community — doctors, lawyers, mechanics, school teachers — to write to their congressmen, and these letters appeared to reflect genuine involvement in the effect on Pittsburgh Plate of foreign competition.[6]

Most of the mail sent on the Reciprocal Trade Act was in some sense stimulated. It is our guess that, among the Eastern and Southern

[6] But note that even this well-worked-out and individualized effort was not enough to disguise the fact of stimulation. The congressman who showed us the material and the present authors were fully aware of the campaign, or we would not be discussing it in this passage. We doubt that there is much stimulated mail which passes undetected.

congressmen on whom we concentrated our attention, Westinghouse, Dow, Monsanto, and Pittsburgh Plate Glass may have stimulated 40 per cent or more of all the mail received on the issue in 1954. In addition, there were the coal, small oil, watch, bicycle, and textile interests, as well as such small groups as the nut- and cherry-growers. All of this mail was protectionist and outnumbered pro-reciprocal-trade mail about ten to one. Mail in favor of reciprocal trade was equally stimulated, and perhaps by even fewer prime movers. Our impression is that three-fourths of all anti-protectionist mail was stimulated directly or indirectly by the League of Women Voters.

Stimulated mail and junk is discounted (some congressmen do not even regard it as mail) because it does not convey the impression that the writer is genuinely involved in the issue.

Congressman to Secretary: Jane, am I right that we haven't received mail from more than five people on this tariff business?

Secretary to Congressman: Yes, except, of course, for the pressure groups.

Stimulated or interest-group mail is the type of communication most likely to be regarded as pressure because it comes close to being an implied threat to mobilize votes against the congressman. Even though, as indicated above, there is every reason for him to discount this threat, it cannot be completely discounted. One lobbyist told us a story from an earlier phase in his career when Speaker William Bankhead said to him, "Look, I've got 400 letters on this bill." "But, Speaker," the lobbyist replied, "you know those are stimulated." "Of course they're stimulated," said Bankhead, "but they're there." The person who has been stimulated to write may be stimulated to vote. Though we are convinced that the likelihood is not great, a shred of suspicion remains. Although the term "pressure" is not often employed about mail, it is almost exclusively applied to such stimulated mail.

The conventional description of congressmen as under pressure carries with it the implication that the communications addressed to them are an undesired burden. But, more often than not, the congressman welcomes communication. One congressman who was having difficulty making up his mind complained that no one came to his office to see him. The only time he saw a lobbyist was when he sought one out! Still others indicated that, on the Reciprocal Trade Act and on other issues, they wanted more communication.

Said one newly appointed assistant: "You know, I was very much surprised at how few representatives of organizations come around to make themselves known." Said another: "I used to be a lobbyist myself. . . . It is a peculiar thing and rather incredible to me — the scarcity of contact with Washington trade-association or labor-union representatives." The assistant of another who was a key figure in the reciprocal-trade fight said: "I absolutely had to beat them over the head at our lobbying organization to find out what I wanted to find out; I had to push and push them on this to get the information." And one congressman, when asked what he had heard from the lobby groups on his side and whether they had pushed him, said: "Hell no, it's just the other way around; it's me calling them up and trying to shaft them to get off their fat rears and get out and do something." To many congressmen, the interest organization is a source of information about the attitudes of significant groups in his public, a source of research data and speech material, and an unofficial propaganda ally to help him put his own case forward. This one speaks of "our lobby."

The reader will recall that, in the chapter on lobbies [not reprinted here], we noted that they became effective when they served as private auxiliaries to congressmen or other persons in a public-policy-forming position. Frequently, the lobby is a service agency for a movement led by or even initiated by a congressman.[7] The congressman who told us that he had to telephone "his" lobby to get them going was not telling us a man-bites-dog story. He was describing a usual state of affairs. For his own career reasons, a congressman wants to be a leader of movements with public appeal. He may define as his profession the mobilization of opinion and the propagation of viewpoints on public issues. Success in that profession, as in any other, depends on creating a product that the public wants and becoming a leading purveyor of it. But, as is also true in business or education, the supplier does not wait passively for wants to appear. He helps create the want. Businessmen spend billions to create wants for their products. Educators educate; they do not

[7] Cf. Stephen K. Bailey, *Congress Makes a Law* (New York: Columbia University Press, 1950). The Full Employment Act, the adoption of which Bailey describes, was conceived in Congress. The liberal congressmen who got it written then pressed the unions and liberal organizations into reluctant support of the measure.

wait to be told what the students want to learn. Congressmen promote movements for legislation. Men like Richard Simpson and Cleveland Bailey, not to mention their precursors, gave form and vitality to protectionism as a program for coping with ills. It was in the United States Congress, not somewhere in the hinterland, that the ideological initiative for protection has been historically centered. And the men who made themselves national figures by taking this initiative led, rather than were led by, hired staff men working in private association offices.

Thus, we note once more that the congressman is not entirely a passive instrument with respect to the communications coming to him. To a large extent, he determines whether he is communicated with, in what manner, and on which side of the issue. We have already seen that businessmen and interest-group representatives tend not to communicate with persons who disagree with them. We recall the case of Congressman Stubborn whose obduracy stopped liberal-trade communications from coming to him; no registered voter, he said, wrote him favoring reciprocal trade. That represents but one side of the coin, however.

The other side is that of congressmen who, by their manner and conduct, communicate their desire for communication. In contrast to Congressman Stubborn, we may consider Congressman Serious Consideration, an indecisive man who called a meeting in his district of people interested in the Reciprocal Trade Act. By publicizing his own indecision, he stimulated his constituents to speak up. The circumstances under which he called the meeting virtually ensured its being dominated by persons with protectionist interests.[8] He voted against HR 1.

Several members of Congress told us: "I tell my people that I want such-and-such a type of letter; otherwise, I won't pay any attention to it." In this way, they produce the letters they want.

Congressman Special, in three months, had, he claimed, received 2,000 letters supporting his position and not one letter opposing it. The reason was that he had spoken up and down the country and his own district on the evils of a low-tariff policy, calling the Reciprocal Trade Act an evil product of intrigue, advocated by Karl Marx and worked out by Harry Dexter White.

---

[8] He asked in effect how the bill would affect his district and heard from industrial interests in his district. He did not ask how it would affect America's world interests. He did not invite foreign spokesmen or foreign-affairs specialists.

It is true, as we have seen in preceding chapters, that a large proportion of businessmen and a surprising proportion of representatives of interest groups communicate perfunctorily with congressmen without first ascertaining their views on the issue in question. But it is also true that, when a congressman's stand becomes known, that fact determines to a large extent what communications get sent to him.

In closing this chapter, we should repeat a previously noted fact which partly explains why pressure groups do not appear to exercise so much pressure with regard to general legislation when viewed from Congress as they appear to when viewed by outside observers. We have pointed out that, during the reciprocal-trade controversy in 1953–1955, lobbyists tended to establish liaison only with the congressmen and senators on their own side. They acted for them as outside men stimulating general public interest in the issue, testifying before committees, or providing staff services for the congressmen and senators. The tactical basis of pressure-group activities seemed to be to assist men already on their side to do the job of persuading fellow legislators. Direct persuasion of uncommitted or opposed congressmen and senators was a minor activity of the lobbies.[9]

[9] Was the reciprocal-trade situation unique or typical in regard to lobbying? It is instructive to note the full range of items on pressures on Congress which appeared in the press during a sample period (July, 1959). Boston industrialist Bernard Goldfine, who had gone out of his way to "maintain good relations" with friends in the national government, was convicted of perjury in refusing to disclose to a Congressional committee all of his activities. The Teamsters Union had been lobbying against labor legislation before Congress. When the lobbyist tried to apply pressure in the classical sense, saying, in effect, "We'll get you," it backfired on him, and he apparently ended up with less support than he had at the beginning (cf. *Time*, July 27, 1959, pp. 12–13). In these same few weeks, Robert Kennedy, then counsel for the Senate Rackets Committee, appeared on several television shows and called for a flood of mail to Congress. His appeal was answered, and thousands of letters poured in. But at the very same time a comparable volume of mail was received in protest against the mistreatment of wild horses! One of the results of the Kennedy appeal reported from Chicago was that so many people were calling to find out who their congressman was that a special telephone service had to be installed. In the meantime, Jack Paar, master of ceremonies of one of the television programs on which Kennedy appeared, shamefacedly reported to his audience that he had telegraphed Senator Javits only to find out that Javits had long been working fervently for the very legislation that Paar urged him to support. During the same period, there was a considerable furor over the pressure tactics of missile manufacturers to obtain contracts. Several weeks of investigation seemed to confirm the fact that little pressure, if any, had been applied, or at least that the people to whom it was

12 *The Press*

The press in its collective sense is perhaps the single most important public voice in the foreign policy field; as informer, interpreter, advocate, critic, it is a continuous and articulate link between foreign policy officials in the government and those people on the outside who follow world events. This last article explores some of these roles of the press in the political process here at home, and its impact on our position internationally.

The Press and Foreign Policy in the United States

Bernard C. Cohen

Increased interest today in the relationship of the press to foreign policy bears witness to the newly recognized importance of a subject with which we all have at least a slight familiarity. Students of international affairs have long been aware of an inescapable connection between the world of the press and the world of foreign

Reprinted from Bernard C. Cohen, "The Press and Foreign Policy in the United States," *Journal of International Affairs*, Vol. X, No. 2, 1956 (*The Press and World Affairs*), pp. 128–37.

---

applied did not regard it as pressure (cf. "Gates Approves Ex-Officers' Jobs," *The New York Times,* July 8, 1959).

All in all, the picture was what we would have expected. Actual pressure is likely to backfire and is a dangerous activity. In the case of the missile program, even a moderate amount of self-serving promotion appeared to generate disproportionate counteractivity. Both Goldfine and the Teamsters Union ended up worse off than they were at the beginning. Kennedy and "Wild-Horse Annie" showed that it was possible to stir up a considerable amount of activity in the form of writing to Congress. But both campaigns of letter-writing seemed to have more head than beer.

policy; but, whenever they moved from awareness to actual discussion of the subject, they demonstrated conflicting opinions — a kind of ambivalence which partially describes the nature of the dilemma posed by press coverage of foreign affairs.

On the one hand, some close observers of American foreign relations over the past generation have frequently wished that the American press would do a more complete job of foreign affairs reporting; they have argued that lack of coverage was a cause as well as a consequence of American disinterest in international relations, and that more discussion of foreign policy in the press would eventually be followed by increased interest and higher levels of information relating to foreign policy among the general public. At the same time, however, other students have taken note of the various occasions through the years when press activity has adversely affected in one way or another the formulation or execution of American foreign policy, and they have argued that the movement of delicate issues of foreign policy from the privacy of the Foreign Offices to the front pages of the newspapers has been accompanied by a noticeable increase in what might be called the popularization of international relations and a corresponding decline in their political efficacy.

These apparently divergent lines of thought have merged, in part with the passage of time, to produce a common body of criticism: the American press has come to be a repeated, if not always an obvious, target for the critical observations of amateur and professional students of American foreign policy. It has not been the only target, to be sure, but it has frequently served as a scapegoat for various imperfections in public opinion on foreign policy and in the conduct of foreign policy itself.

It is not too much to say that both of these views of the press and foreign policy, and their common burden of criticism, are oversimplified versions of reality, and that the renewed interest in the role played by the press in the process of foreign policy-making in the United States is a necessary first step in the direction of a more accurate appraisal. Much study, not only of the press itself but also of the entire process of foreign policy-making, has to be undertaken before we can have any confidence in our mastery of the subject. In the light of our present knowledge, it is somewhat reckless to make positive statements about the influence of the press on foreign policy; yet there are still some tentative hypotheses and suggestive propositions which can be advanced here and which might contribute to future study of the subject. The most important of these hypotheses, one which is both implicit and explicit in the following discussion, is that the press has become an integral factor in the process of foreign policy-making in the United States today — a factor so deeply involved and of such central concern that its elimination would radically and fundamentally alter the very character of that process. The press functions in the political process not like a pressure group, which may exert influence here or force the development of policy there; it works, rather, like the bloodstream in the human body, enabling the process that we are familiar with today to continue on, by linking up all the widely scattered parts, putting them in touch with one another, and supplying them with political and intellectual nourishment.

I

The relationship of the press to American foreign policy-making is exceedingly complex; in fact, generalizations about the influence of the press are difficult to formulate in view of the rich variety of behavior that makes up this relationship. "The press" itself is composed of many different people and groups of people; it serves many different functions in the foreign policy-making process; and thus it can have many different effects on that process or on the behavior of the other persons and institutions involved with the process. Each of these differences deserves some exploration, for they help to explain the various kinds of influence the press exerts on foreign policy.

The press has its effect on foreign policy-making through the printed word; thus the definition of "the press" must be wide enough to include not only the many different newspapers in the country, but also all the different people whose decisions determine the foreign affairs content of each newspaper. "Reporting" is crucial here, though it is only part of the communications process. Some foreign affairs reporting is done by special diplomatic or foreign affairs correspondents assigned by their papers not only to Washington but also to every other major capital in the world. Less affluent papers may have one or two foreign correspondents, and depend on an ordinary reporter for all of their Washington news, domestic and foreign. Most newspapers, however, rely almost exclusively for their foreign affairs news on the major wire services, whose correspondents cover every important source of foreign policy news at home and abroad. It is, in fact, the heavy dependence on the wire services which accounts for the large degree of uniformity in the foreign affairs coverage of American newspapers.[1]

The attitude of foreign affairs correspondents in Washington toward policy-making deserves brief mention here, since the character and substance of their reporting depend to some extent on the way they visualize the crucial processes through which foreign policy is formulated.[2] Generally, these Washington reporters regard the executive branch, and particularly the State Department, as the leader — the initiator and responsible agent — in foreign policy-making; they view the foreign policy role of Congress principally as a brake on executive action. In these circumstances they tend to be oriented chiefly to the executive branch and to follow its side of the policy-making story more closely. Of equal significance, these reporters do not think of themselves as having direct influence on policy formation; and they are for the most part reluctant to become involved in the policy process, either as direct consultants or as instruments for the launching of trial balloons. They try wherever possible to preserve the customary distinction between objective reporting and editorializing, although they admit that the news columns and the increasing use of background stories and interpretative articles may have some influence on policy and public opinion.

In addition to "reporting," "editing" is also an important determinant of foreign affairs content in the press. This means that the study of the effects of the press on foreign policy properly includes the people on the staffs of newspapers and the wire services who help to edit stories, determine layout, allocate headline space, and otherwise assign priorities among various types of local, state, regional, national, and international news. In other words, whatever consequences for American foreign policy the American press may have on any particular occasion are a function not only of the kind and caliber of the reporting that takes place, but equally of the

[1] For an interesting study of news from abroad, see *The Flow of the News,* A Study by the International Press Institute, Zurich, the International Press Institute, 1953.

[2] This paragraph is based upon interviews with over forty foreign affairs reporters in Washington, D.C.; the interviews were conducted by Theodore Kolderie and Joachim Schumacher, as part of the Graduate Research Seminar of the Woodrow Wilson School of Public and International Affairs, Princeton University, during 1953–54. The Seminar was a catalyst in the development of other ideas on the press and foreign policy-making which have found their way into this article.

whole context of news and its presentation, which endows events with varying degrees of salience and immediacy.

Despite the reluctance of newspapermen to be "drawn into" the process of foreign policy-making, the press is nevertheless intimately involved; one way of gauging the extent of this involvement is to examine the different functions that the press performs in the field of foreign policy formulation. In the first place, the press *communicates.* That is to say, it transmits information both of a policy character (from those who are in the midst of events and have policy responsibilities in the government) and also of an opinion character (from those whose views on policy are thought to have significance). However, in making decisions about what information to transmit, how to say it and how to "play" it, the press is clearly interposing judgments about the significance of policies and opinions between the various producers and consumers of news. The criteria according to which these judgments are made may be conscious or unconscious; but from the insistence of newspapermen that reporting is an exercise in objectivity one is led to suspect that their judgments are based on criteria which are obscure even to themselves. Often there is a close correspondence between the judgments of importance made this way by the press, and the judgments made by foreign policy-makers or by other observers; but there are numerous occasions where the "news sense" of the press leads it away from serious issues toward spectacular ones.

Interpretation is also a well-recognized function of the press, although it is generally performed explicitly not by news-gathering reporters but by special columnists or analysts. Some newspapers can afford to keep their own interpretive writers, like James Reston of *The New York Times* or Roscoe Drummond of the *New York Herald Tribune;* others print columns which are distributed by syndicates. Just as the wire services are responsible for much of the uniformity in coverage of foreign affairs news, syndicated columns may be a factor tending toward the standardization of foreign policy interpretation in a nation without a truly national newspaper.[3] With the growing complexity and subtlety of international affairs since the end of the Second World War, the press has increasingly felt a

[3] Other factors, undoubtedly more important, are the national radio and television networks, and the national news magazines. The news columns of the papers also help to standardize interpretation by reporting the views of leading public figures.

need to supplement news columns with columns of background information, explanation, and interpretation of the meaning of events. This is a deliberate, conscious effort to give some structure to policy issues for a vast, inexpert audience, in contrast to the unconscious structuring that often is part of the straight communication function.

Advocacy is another of the major functions of the press. Newspapers generally lend their support to foreign policies in their editorial columns, although there are still some papers here and there in which the advocacy of policy is a feature of the front page and the news columns. There is ample evidence in election results that newspaper advocacy is not always effective with respect to public opinion, but this is not to say that advocacy by the press is therefore without importance. In the eyes of many government officials, the press represents an enlightened and articulate section of the general public; in these circumstances press support of a particular policy may assume important weight when expressions of public opinion are examined for their political significance.

In addition to these three major functions which the American press performs in the process of foreign policy-making, a minor one deserves some notice: this is the function of *initiation*. Sometimes the press, or more accurately a particular newspaper or a particular correspondent, is responsible for the government's consideration of specific policies to meet specific problems. This does not happen often, since few papers have sufficient prestige to start an important chain of events, and since most newspapermen are reluctant to "compromise" their independence and objectivity by crossing the line into policy-making territory. But every once in a while a reporter who has the confidence of a policy-maker may start him thinking along a new line of policy, or a newspaper that can afford to undertake an independent study of a policy area may bring that area to the attention of top policy-makers more effectively than the subordinate government personnel who are in charge of it. Indeed, when their own internal channels of communication present overwhelming obstacles, these government officials may deliberately seek the assistance of the press in publicizing issues so that the top-level policy-makers will be stimulated into taking policy action.

In the performance of all of these functions, the press is playing an important role in the political process: it is helping to create or shape the outlines of foreign policy issues in the minds of the general public, of organized groups, and of government officials more or less remote or removed from these particular issues; and almost at the same time it is helping to provide policy-makers with some image of "public opinion" on the issues thus structured. A decentralized political process requires an effective communications network; in the United States, a large part of this network is supplied by a public press which is also decentralized. In these circumstances the opportunities for foreign policy influence by the press are many and varied.

It is not surprising, then, that close examination of the ways in which the press may affect United States foreign policy, like a study of the constituent parts of "the press" and its diverse functions, reveals a complexity that is generally ignored or overlooked in casual discussion of the press and foreign policy. To take the reporting aspect of the press operation for a moment, there can be no simple description of how foreign policy reporting from Washington affects the conduct of American foreign affairs. The reporting job may affect the detailed conduct of foreign affairs in very many ways — ways which at one time may be thought desirable and at another time not. For example, press scrutiny of foreign policy activity on the governmental level may have the effect of bringing a new foreign policy into the market place of ideas, where its substantive merit and its political appropriateness can be tested. But it may also have the effect of destroying public support for the policy by demonstrating its weaknesses, even though there may be no readily available substitute policy and even though the proposed one may have been better than no policy at all. These may be rather obvious virtues and vices which are inherent in the work of any effective foreign affairs reporter; yet they are also illustrative of the fact that more than one consequence may flow from any given manner of press handling of a foreign policy issue, and that it is difficult to generalize about these consequences in the abstract, without reference to a specific situation.

Let us pursue for a moment longer this question of press scrutiny, in view of the recurrent interest in whether the press precipitates policy commitments or diplomatic actions by publicizing issues. Much of the effect of publicity on policy or action depends on the over-all character of the publicity and on the nature of the "story" which is thought to be of public interest. If publicity takes the form of an exposé, a revelation, it may have a restraining influence by causing policy-makers to hesitate for fear of provoking an adverse public, or perhaps even Congressional, reaction; if the policy issues are publicized on the initiative of the foreign policy officials themselves, the publicity may give them the necessary public support so they can take bolder policy action; if publicity is given to diplomatic positions at critical stages of negotiations, it may destroy the possibilities of compromise, or it may force a commitment of some unplanned kind.

The press might perhaps be likened to a musical instrument, which can be played differently to achieve different effects. The most successful public relations have generally been the work of people who understood the instrument-like variability of the press and who shared the expert newsman's intuitive ability to define what is "news" in any situation. Ambitious politicians have frequently made the most of their knowledge and ability in these respects, to their personal gain. They have realized that the press is not simply an automatic transmission belt which can be counted on to carry "all" information from political sources to the public, but rather that newspapermen often have to make judgments and choices as to the significance of information and the emphasis to be placed on it, and that these judgments can be directed or influenced in various ways.[4] The State Department and the Defense Department, however, and other foreign policy-making agencies of the government as well, have frequently tended to regard the behavior of the press as a disaster rather than an opportunity and have tried to protect themselves by keeping at a distance. As a result, when newspapermen have found obstacles in the path of their direct access to the sources of important information, foreign policy publicity has sometimes taken the form of sudden revelations, or incorrect speculations, with all their undesirable consequences. In other words, the unhappy effects of publicizing issues of foreign policy may on occasion be as much the responsibility of foreign policy officials who do not understand the potentialities of press coverage of foreign policy as they are the responsibility of an "irresponsible" press that tries to obtain public policy information by one means or another.

As long as the press can endow an event with political significance by the process of giving it wide currency, this question of the character of press coverage of foreign policy is a serious one. And it will

[4] At the height of Senator McCarthy's prestige, for example, thoughtful newsmen were beginning to be uncomfortably aware of the part they had unintentionally played in the Senator's rapid political rise.

not soon disappear, since public interest in foreign policy is likely to remain at least at present levels, entailing the prospect of constant, if not increasing, press coverage of the subject. It seems appropriate, then, for us to try to acquire more specific and detailed information about the press's relationship to the foreign policy-making process, so that our efforts to ameliorate "irresponsible" journalism in the foreign policy field can take the form of concrete and realistic proposals rather than collective hand-wringing or pious exhortations.

II

Recent events, as well as the present context of international life, pose two important problems relating to the press and foreign policy which are of a different order from those discussed above. Up to this point we have been concerned with the influence of the press on the conduct and content of United States foreign policy; here we are interested in the effects that the press might have on America's position internationally. What are the consequences for national security of press discussion on crucial questions of foreign policy? And what difficulties for American policy-makers are raised by the fact that policy-makers abroad look to the American press for clues to our official attitudes and intentions in the foreign policy sphere?

The relationship of the press to national security is especially intricate, since it involves not only the difficult problems of evaluating all the possible uses and meanings of information, but also the emotionally significant subject of democratic values. As a general proposition, it would seem that in the normal course of events the security consequences of press behavior are a matter of less immediate concern than the political and policy consequences discussed above. The wartime situation is different, of course, but there is little evidence that in peacetime the American press coverage of the details of our foreign policy jeopardizes national security. True, one can always discover instances where the press has uncovered (or been given) "classified information" of one sort or another, but there is quite a gap between that situation and any demonstration that the national security has been perceptibly weakened thereby. The press as a group is as concerned about the security of the country as any other group. At the same time, newspapermen are likely — for obvious reasons — to be among the most vigorous defenders of the freedom of the press and also of the proposition that democracy can flourish only where the people are informed on public policy. In this sense it is possible to argue, with some justification, that American

national security is on balance enhanced rather than weakened by
the activities of the press in bringing intimate problems of foreign
policy to the public forum. Detailed discussions of defense estimates,
for example, or of the development of ballistic missiles, or of the size
and composition of the Air Force, may even have as positive a value
externally as they do internally. At home the press coverage of —
and contribution to — the discussion of these subjects may serve to
end protracted bureaucratic debate, to consolidate and enlarge the
area of agreement, to facilitate decision, and to speed actual work
on programs. Abroad, it would be a mistake to assume that all
knowledge of our "secrets" serves to weaken our security; depending
on the nature of the "secret," press discussion of the matter may
even strengthen our position by leading other nations to recalculate
their own vulnerabilities.[5]

Many of these same considerations apply also to the second question raised above: what policy-making difficulties grow from the fact
that policy-makers abroad seek out our official attitudes and intentions in our daily press? There is no question that the press can
make life difficult for American policy-makers, and that many of
them would prefer a far greater measure of privacy for the conduct
of their official business. Yet there is nothing new or unique about
this situation, nor is it necessarily true that these difficulties are so
disturbing to the conduct of foreign policy as to warrant a change
in the present condition of affairs. Policy-makers in many nations
scrutinize the press of many other nations for indications of their
foreign policy attitudes and intentions. The United States press, in
fact, poses problems for the United States government that are not
much different from those posed for other governments by their
public presses. One might even argue that a free press in a democracy — because of the inevitably conflicting and contradictory
"official" reports that are always in circulation — creates less of a
governmental fish bowl than does a controlled press in a dictatorship
that forbids public expression of a wide range of attitudes.

Furthermore, it is easy to imagine situations where American
foreign policy interests are furthered by press disclosure of official
attitudes and intentions. This is particularly true where there may
be danger involved in an incorrect assessment of our intentions by

[5] Cf., in this connection, Bernard Brodie, "Military Demonstrations and
Disclosure of New Weapons," *World Politics*, Vol. 5, No. 3, April 1953, pp.
281–301.

another nation.[6] Where we desire to bluff, however, or perhaps have no alternative between bluffing or giving up one of our interests, the press may undermine our position by forcing some kind of statement of intention and thus disclosing the substance of the bluff. There is a challenge to policy-makers here to see if they can devise new policy means to avoid these kinds of situations.[7]

Foreign scrutiny of the American press may be a source of embarrassment to American policy-makers in another kind of situation where the policy-makers have made public statements designed for domestic consumption that prove to be a source of irritation or offence to foreign observers. In these respects, however, the press is little more than a transmission belt, reporting the policy utterances of prominent officials. Whatever problems are raised by these occurrences are traceable more to domestic politics and political personalities than to the press itself.

III

Perhaps the major — if obvious — conclusions to be drawn from these comments are that the foreign policy consequences of the American press are varied, and that all the other factors in the foreign policy-making process share in the responsibility for these consequences. This is not to lift from the shoulders of the press its responsibility for its own behavior. A corollary to the freedom of the press is that the press must do a careful job of policing itself, remaining ever watchful of its own responsibilities to the ethics of the profession and to the national interest, widely defined. But perhaps we should not expect from the press any better understanding of the web of relationships that comprise the policy-making process than we expect from other participants in the process; and on this score we can only hope that greater understanding will accompany the further development of knowledge.

[6] The MacArthur hearings certainly revealed many hitherto secret aspects of official United States attitudes and intentions at the time of the Korean war. It is possible, however, that in the process of revealing them the United States managed to set the Chinese Communists and the Russians straight in an otherwise confused situation, and thus helped to keep the war in Korea limited.

[7] The official American policy of keeping the Chinese Communists guessing as to our intentions in the event of an attack by them on Quemoy off the Chinese mainland has so far withstood all efforts by the press and others to secure an elaboration. Cf. also William W. Kaufmann, "The Requirements of Deterrence," in William W. Kaufmann, ed., *Military Policy and National Security* (Princeton: Princeton University Press, 1956).